MAKERS
OF MODERN BRITAIN

MAKERS
OF MODERN BRITAIN

Richard Tames

Batsford Academic and Educational Ltd London

Typeset by Tek Art Ltd,
and printed in Great Britain by
R. J. Acford
Chichester, Sussex
for the publishers
Batsford Academic and Educational Ltd,
an imprint of B. T. Batsford Ltd,
4 Fitzhardinge Street
London W1H 0AH

ISBN 0 7134 4055 4

Contents

ADAM,
Robert
(1728-92)

The most talented member of a family of
Scottish architects, Robert Adam was one of
the leaders of the mid-eighteenth-century
"classical revival". He was, in his own words,
"a very promising young man". Educated at
Edinburgh University, Adam, like many young
architects of his day, completed his training
by taking an extended journey through France,
Italy and Dalmatia (modern Yugoslavia),

Robert Adam, portrait attributed to George Willison,
c. 1770-5.

The stairs at Osterley House.

making drawings of ancient temples and
public buildings. Adam himself made a series
of drawings, later published, of the palace of
the Roman emperor, Diocletian, at Spalato
(Split). His career was chiefly concerned with
the design of town and country houses. In his
designs he made great use of classical devices
and motifs, such as arcades and alcoves,
decorated with plaster ornamentation painted
in delicate pastel colours. Adam was one of
the first designers to take an interest in the
overall décor of a house — not merely the
building, but its decoration, furniture and
carpets as well. Indeed, thirty years after
Adam's death, a critic wrote that his "success
arose chiefly from his knowledge of detail and
his minute and elaborate taste". Osterley
House, to the west of London, is a good

example of his work. Others can be found at Portland Place and Fitzroy Square, in London's West End. The Adelphi, an ambitious residential block off the Strand, which all but ruined his family firm, was demolished in the 1930s. Horace Walpole, the writer who considered Adam's work "all gingerbread", dismissed the Adelphi as "warehouses laced down the seams". The best of Adam's country houses are at Kedleston in Derbyshire and Kenwood at Hampstead. He also helped to design the New Town of Edinburgh, the University and Charlotte Square being based on his plans. But he was never commissioned to design a public building in London.

ALBERT,
Prince Consort
(1819-61)

Albert of Saxe-Coburg-Gotha married Queen Victoria, his first cousin, in 1840. The Queen came to depend almost entirely on his advice and judgment and he became, in effect, her chief political adviser. As Charles Greville noted in his *Memoirs*, "The Prince is become so identified with the Queen, that they are one person (and as he likes and she dislikes business, it is obvious that while she has the title he is really discharging the functions of

Victoria and Albert — domestic bliss and the outdoor life.

The Albert Hall and, left, the Albert Memorial.

the sovereign. He is King to all intents and purposes)." Albert's serious manner did not win him admirers in fashionable society, but political leaders came to respect his ability and integrity, though they sometimes thought him meddlesome. A man of wide interests, he was the moving spirit behind the Great Exhibition of 1851, a keen supporter of many charitable and scientific projects and a lover of the outdoor life, introducing the Queen to the beauties of the Scottish Highlands. Devotion to duty undermined the Prince Consort's health and he died of typhoid at the age of 42, leaving behind a grief-stricken Queen and a nation which now revered him as "Albert the Good". He is commemorated by the Albert Hall and the nearby Albert Memorial and also by the Christmas tree, which he introduced to England from his native Germany. His last words are said to have been: "I have had wealth, rank and power, but, if these were all I had, how wretched I should be."

ARKWRIGHT,
Sir Richard
(1732-92)

Arkwright must be numbered among the founders of the modern industrial system, not because he was a great inventor, but because he was a versatile and energetic businessman with the ability to raise capital and organize labour as well as to grasp the importance of the new technology of textile manufacture. A self-made man, with scarcely any formal education, Arkwright began as a barber in Bolton and ended as a Knight and High Sheriff of Derbyshire, with a personal fortune

Sir Richard Arkwright, portrait by Joseph Wright of Derby, 1790.

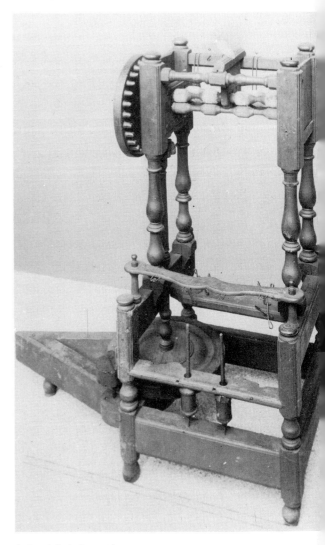

Arkwright's invention.

of £500,000. Arkwright's "water-frame", patented in 1769, was almost certainly not his own original invention, and the patent was cancelled in 1785, but he used it to revolutionize the manufacture of cotton textiles. The great advantage of the frame was that it could spin a cotton thread strong enough to be used for the warp (vertical threads) as well as the weft. This made it possible to dispense with the more expensive wool or linen warp and to make all-cotton cloth. Because the frame was powered by water, and from 1790 by steam, cotton spinners no longer worked in their own homes but instead were concentrated together in factories to tend the powered machinery. At Cromford in Derbyshire and at New Lanark in Scotland, where Robert Owen was later to work, Arkwright pioneered the new methods of the industrial age and, by his success, inspired a whole generation of entrepreneurs.

"Arkwright was a tremendous worker and a man of marvellous energy, ardor and application in business. At one period of his life he was usually engaged in the severe and continuous labours involved by the organization and conduct of his numerous manufactories, from four in the morning until nine at night. At fifty years of age he set to work to learn English grammar . . . . When he travelled to save time he went at great speed, drawn by four horses . . . ." (Samuel Smiles, *Self-help*, 1859)

ARNOLD,
Rev Thomas
(1795-1842)

Dr Arnold was the most famous headmaster of the nineteenth century. His reforms at Rugby School (1828-42) were widely imitated by other public schools and, in the course of time, came to influence many aspects of the education system as a whole. Before Arnold, the public school curriculum consisted almost entirely of Greek and Latin; Arnold added such subjects as modern history, mathematics

Thomas Arnold, portrait by Thomas Phillips, 1839.

and modern languages. He was also a firm believer in the value of organized games. But he placed the highest value on the development of moral qualities, asserting that the main aim of a public school education should be to produce Christian gentlemen with a strong sense of duty. For this reason, he placed great emphasis on the prefectorial system which gave senior boys a large measure of responsibility for the organization of the school. He was an idealist and, at the same time, a realist; as he wrote at the time of his appointment as Headmaster: "My object will be, if possible, to form Christian men, for Christian boys I can scarcely hope to make." Walter Bagehot, the Victorian writer, said of him that: "The influence of Arnold's teaching on the majority of his pupils was probably very vague, but very good." A vivid picture of Arnold's days at Rugby is to be found in

Thomas Hughes' novel *Tom Brown's School-days*, Arnold died shortly after being appointed Professor of Modern History at Oxford. His methods of education affected the outlook of generations of England's social and political elite. His son, Matthew Arnold (1822-88), was to become a distinguished poet and literary critic and an influential inspector of schools.

"Dr. Arnold was almost indisputably an admirable master for a common English boy — the small, apple-eating animal whom we know. He worked, he pounded . . . into the boy a belief, or at any rate a floating, confused conception, that there are great subjects, that there are strange problems, that knowledge has an indefinite value, that life is a serious and solemn thing." (Walter Bagehot, 1826-77)

View of the Southern Schools and Dormitories of Rugby School from the Playground.

ATTLEE,
Clement Richard
(1883-1967)

Educated at Haileybury and Oxford, Attlee was converted to socialism as a result of doing social work in London's East End. Having lectured at Ruskin College and the London School of Economics, he was commissioned into the South Lancashire Regiment in 1914 and served in the Middle East and France, ending the war as a major. After serving as Mayor of Stepney (1919-20), Attlee entered the Commons as Labour MP for Limehouse in 1922. His experiences as a member of the Simon Commission, which visited India in 1927, convinced him of the strength of the nationalist movement and were therefore to exert a powerful influence on his views twenty years later.

When the Labour Party split in 1931, Attlee refused to join MacDonald's National Government. In 1935 he was elected party leader, in succession to the ineffectual Lansbury, and devoted himself to restoring the party's unity and confidence.

In 1940 Attlee joined Churchill's Coalition War Cabinet and was officially recognized as Deputy Prime Minister in 1942. Labour's election victory in 1945 made him Prime Minister and as such he oversaw the nationalization of the railways, coal mines, gas, electricity and steel industries, the establishment of the National Health Service and the transition to independence of India and Pakistan. After Labour's defeat in 1951, Attlee

Attlee addressing Trade Union delegates in Manchester, 1947.

The Rt. Hon. C. R. Attlee OM. CH.

YOU CAN TRUST MR. ATTLEE

Election poster, May 1955.

remained Leader of the Opposition until 1955, when he was created an Earl.

A skilled party manager, well able to reconcile differences between his supporters, Attlee was above all a brisk and business-like chairman. Despite his academic and upper-middle-class background, he was more interested in the practice of socialism than in its theory and doctrines. Attlee himself admitted that "I have none of the qualities which create publicity" and Churchill dismissed him as "a sheep in sheep's clothing". Modest, kindly and reserved, Attlee did often seem colourless compared to Churchill, but he was no less effective in getting things done.

AUSTEN,
Jane
(1775-1817)

The seventh child of a Hampshire clergyman, Jane Austen, having been educated by her father, lived quietly in that county for most of her life. As a novelist she wrote about the world she knew, the world of respectable rural England, peopled by the educated and the elegant. The American writer, Emerson, thought her outlook "pinched and narrow". And Jane Austen described herself as "the most unlearned and uninformed female who ever dared to be an authoress". Villagers and

Jane Austen, a watercolour drawing by her sister, Cassandra, c. 1801.

Ile began to compliment her on her improved looks.

An illustration by Hugh Thompson from *Persuasion*.

life — the meaning of a glance, a letter or an unexpected meeting.

Sense and Sensibility (1811), *Pride and Prejudice* (1813), *Mansfield Park* (1814) and *Emma* (1816) were published in her lifetime; *Northanger Abbey* and *Persuasion* after her death. Although Sir Walter Scott greatly admired her work, she had little influence on other writers in her time and it was not until the twentieth century that her genius was fully recognized. Jane Austen's view of her craft is perhaps best conveyed by an exchange between two characters in *Northanger Abbey*:

'And what are you reading, Miss . . .?' 'Oh, it is only a novel.' . . . or, in short, only some work in which the most thorough knowledge of human nature, the happiest delineation of its varieties, the liveliest effusions of wit and humour are conveyed to the world in the best chosen language.

The novelist Somerset Maugham (1874-1965) put the point a little differently:

Nothing very much happens in her books, and yet, when you come to the bottom of a page, you eagerly turn it to learn what will happen next. Nothing much does and again you eagerly turn the page. The novelist who has the power to achieve this has the most precious gift a novelist can possess.

servants rarely appear in her novels as characters in their own right. Only parsons and officers of the armed forces appear to have any duties beyond the cultivated appreciation of nature and society which fills the daily lives of the leisured class. Most of her characters seem to exist only so that she can observe their manners and behaviour.

Jane Austen wrote with a firm sense of right and wrong and a keen awareness of the weaknesses which make people both ridiculous and pathetic. She admired good manners and detested insincerity. She excelled in portraying the small dramas of everyday

"One half of the world cannot understand the pleasures of the other." (Jane Austen, *Emma*)

"I do not want people to be very agreeable, as it saves me the trouble of liking them a great deal." (Jane Austen, Letters, 1798)

BAIRD,
John Logie
(1888-1946)

The inventor of television was born at Helensburgh, Scotland. After studying electrical engineering in Glasgow, and failing in several business ventures, Baird set up an experimental workshop in Hastings in 1922. Despite poverty and poor health, he developed a primitive television apparatus from such everyday items as torch lenses, darning needles and a biscuit tin. On 26 January 1926 he gave the first ever public demonstration of television in a rented room in London's Soho. In 1927 he achieved a television link-up between London and Glasgow, and in the following year he demonstrated both colour television and a link-up between London and New York and a ship in mid-Atlantic. In 1929 Baird's system was adopted on an experimental basis by the BBC. Regular broadcasts began in 1936, but in 1937 the BBC switched to a television system developed by EMI-Marconi.

Baird with an experimental colour TV, 1938.

BALDWIN,
Stanley
(1867-1947)

Educated at Harrow and Cambridge, Baldwin succeeded his father, a wealthy iron manufacturer, as MP for Bewdley (Worcestershire), his birthplace, in 1908. Entering the Cabinet as President of the Board of Trade in 1921, Baldwin played a leading part in the momentous Carlton Club meeting (19 October 1922) which led to the break-up of Lloyd George's Coalition Government. After serving briefly as Chancellor of the Exchequer,

Stanley Baldwin.

Baldwin held the office of Prime Minister in 1923, from 1924 to 1929 and from 1935 to 1937. As Lord President of the Council in Ramsay MacDonald's National Government (1931-35), he was one of the most influential men in the Cabinet, even when not Prime Minister.

Baldwin liked to present himself to the public as an Englishman's Englishman — not clever but moderate, calm and resolute in times of difficulty. Indeed, he once described himself as "steeped in tradition and impervious to new ideas". He truly believed in democracy and compromise, but his skilful handling of the General Strike (1926) and the abdication crisis (1936) showed the shrewd politician behind the pipe-smoking man of goodwill. Criticized during his lifetime for failing to recognize the threat of Nazi power, Baldwin was, in fact, conscious of Britain's need to re-arm, but realized that public support for this was lacking.

Baldwin's description of his family firm shows well the ideal of the humane, if rather easy-going, England in which he believed:

> It was a place where strikes and lockouts were unknown. It was a place where the fathers and grandfathers of the men then working there had worked. . . .It was a place where nobody ever 'got the sack' . . . and where a large number of old gentlemen used to spend their days sitting on the handles of wheelbarrows, smoking their pipes.

Lord Beaverbrook said of Baldwin that he was

> a well-meaning man of indifferent judgment who, whether he did right or wrong, was always sustained by a belief that he was acting for the best.

BANKS,
Sir Joseph
(1743–1820)

Sir Joseph Banks was the most important scientist of his day, not on account of his own discoveries, which were few, but because he used his great influence and fortune to promote and finance the work of fellow scientists. Educated at Eton and Oxford, Banks became a keen botanist and in his youth sailed as a ship's naturalist to Labrador and Newfoundland. He then accompanied Captain Cook's *Endeavour* on its historic voyage to the South Pacific, and gathered an immense quantity of plants, insects and other specimens. He returned to find himself a celebrity. In 1778 he was elected President of the Royal Society, a position he held for the

Sir Joseph Banks.

The Royal Society in 1807-8. Joseph Banks is portrayed ninth from the left, standing.

next 42 years. His home became a meeting-place for scientists and men of affairs, and Banks, a personal friend of George III, took the lead in such projects as the establishment of the Botanic Gardens at Kew and the colonization of Australia. He was also responsible for the introduction of merino sheep into Britain and the introduction of the cultivation of tea in India.

BEAVERBROOK, Lord (William Maxwell Aitken) (1879-1964)

The son of a Canadian Presbyterian minister, Max Aitken was a self-made millionaire by the age of 30. In 1910 he emigrated to England, joined forces with the Conservative leader, Bonar Law, a fellow Canadian, and within three months was elected as a Conservative MP, being knighted the following year. In

Max Aitken, Lord Beaverbrook.

DAILY EXPRESS

No. 8122.   FRIDAY, MAY 7, 1926   ONE PENNY.

Train Services Improve.
FEWER DELAYS FOR WORKERS.

Many more trains were running yesterday in the London district and also in a number of the provincial centres.

It was a comparatively easy business on some of the London suburban lines for people to get to and from work. This, coupled with the fact that the immense road traffic was far better controlled, prevented the delays which most people experienced in reaching their offices on the first two days.

The following are the reports from the companies:—

G.W.R.—Trains between London, Ealing, Slough, Reading, Oxford and Worcester. Milk traffic handled satisfactorily.

Southern.—More than 330 trains in operation. Main line services to Bognor, Dover, Brighton, Portsmouth, Ramsgate, Hastings and Reading. Services steadily improving. Every important main line station has some service to London. Electric trains in London district at regular intervals.

L.N.E.R.—Considerable improvement in all suburban traffic. Service in each direction on all main lines and important branches. Expresses running between York and Newcastle and Doncaster and London.

L.M.S.—All milk trains from stations for delivery without a hitch. Skeleton suburban service in operation.

Metropolitan—Fifteen minutes service each way between Baker-street and Harrow. Hourly train between Baker-street, Rickmansworth and Uxbridge. Regular services on Northern route of the Inner Circle.

Omnibus Set on Fire.

Rowdyism broke out in the vicinity of the Elephant and Castle yesterday morning. A large crowd of "Roughs" gathered and one section of them stopped an omnibus which was going along St. George's road.

They ordered the passengers, driver and conductor out of the vehicle and then set the omnibus on fire. It blazed furiously for some time but the fire was eventually put out by the fire brigade.

A large detachment of mounted police was later rushed to the district and complete order was restored.

Steelworkers' Return.

Over ninety per cent. of the men employed at the large steel works of Messrs. Whiteheads at Newport, Mon., returned to work yesterday, and both hot and cold mills are running normally.

Taxi Cab Strike.

London taxicab drivers have decided to join the strike. The decision was taken at a meeting on Wednesday night but there were many taxicabs on the streets yesterday.

THE INEVITABLE END.

By now the majority of the strikers recognise that failure is upon them.

Mr. Bromley, the Labour leader, has admitted in the House of Commons that they cannot prevail against the full resources of the Government. Those resources will be fully employed.

The Trade Union Congress will perfect truth define the issue as *for* or *against* the strike.

The vast majority of the nation including most of the strikers are against it. The British public are on the side of Parliamentary Government.

Only Trade Union discipline has saved the strike from total collapse. Its early breakdown is inevitable.

Buckrose By-Election.

The result of the by-election in the Buckrose Division of Yorkshire (following the retirement of Vice-Admiral Sir Guy Gaunt) was as follows:—

Major A. N. Braithwaite (C.) 12,099
Sir Harry Verney (L.) 10,537
Mr. H. C. Laycock (Soc.) 2,131

Conservative majority 1,562

The General Election result was:—
Sir Guy Gaunt (C.) 13,966 ; Mr. H. A. Briggs (L.) 10,962. Conservative majority 3,004.

Bank Rate Unchanged.

There was no change in the Bank Rate yesterday.

London Theatres.

Most of the London theatres are "carrying on."

Premier's Message.

The following message from the Prime Minister was included in the second number of the "British Gazette."

"Constitutional Government is being attacked. Let all good citizens whose livelihood and labour have thus been put in peril bear with fortitude and patience the hardships with which they have been so suddenly confronted. Stand behind the Government, who are doing their part, confident that you will co-operate in the measures they have undertaken to preserve the liberties and privileges of the people of these islands. The laws of England are the people's birthright. The laws are in your keeping. You have made Parliament their guardian. The general strike is a challenge to Parliament and is the road to anarchy and ruin. . . ."
Stanley Baldwin."

Strikers Return to Work.

Numbers of strikers returned to work in various parts of the country yesterday and it is anticipated that their example will be followed by others to-day.

Transport workers in Grimsby reported themselves for duty yesterday morning. The tramcar services in the town are now the only section of road transport affected by the strike.

Seventy per cent. of the Liverpool tramwaymen returned to duty and services ran normally during the day.

Dock-keepers at Liverpool also reported for work and the electricians employed at Liverpool's main power house resumed their duties.

The number of strikers returning at the Wolverton carriage works of the London, Midland & Scottish Railway is increasing and 180 men are now at work.

Clerks and carpenters are working at McCorquodale's Printing Works, Wolverton.

Fulham Palace.

Fulham Palace has been offered by the Bishop of London as a neutral meeting place for future negotiations to end the trouble in the coal industry.

The Bishop announced that he had made that offer in a letter to Mr. J. H. Thomas, M.P., at a public meeting of intercession held in the Queens Hall.

"The raising of the standard of living of the poorest" said the Bishop, "is a worthy object, but past experience has shown that it is not to be attained by any short cuts."

The Bishop of London declared that he had been made to feel a certain amount of bitterness towards those responsible for calling the strike, by the spectacle of little working girls having to walk six or seven miles to and from their places of employment.

Cricket.

Surrey v Glamorgan (Oval).
Glamorgan 264 all out
Surrey 196 for 4
(Shepherd not 117)
Essex v Australians (Leyton)
Australians 532 for 8
(Macartney 148 out,
Woodfull 201 out)
Lancashire v Worcestershire
(Manchester)
Worcestershire 194
Lancashire 282 for 7
H. Tyldesley 87 out
Cambridge v Yorkshire
(Cambridge)
Yorkshire 178 & 185 for 9
Cambridge 176 all out

Saklatvala Goes to Prison.
TWO MONTHS' SENTENCE

Mr. Saklatvala, the Parsee Communist M.P. for Battersea close to go to prison for two months at Bow-street Police-court yesterday rather than find two sureties for his good behaviour.

He was brought before Sir Chartres Biron, the chief Metropolitan magistrate, on remand, to show cause why he should not enter into recognizances and find sureties to be of good behaviour and keep the peace. The proceedings arose out of an alleged seditious speech, which it was stated Mr. Saklatvala had given at the May Day Labour demonstration in Hyde Park.

Police were on duty outside the Court-house and no crowd was permitted to collect. The public part of the court was filled with interested listeners. Among them was the wife of the defendant.

An order was made by the Magistrate that Mr. Saklatvala should find two sureties or as an alternative go to prison for two months.

"It is absolutely impossible for me to comply with that decision and to find the two sureties," declared Mr. Saklatvala.

Sir Chartres Biron : "Very well, you must go to prison for two months. No reasonable man can doubt but that the speech you delivered was seditious. Coming at this moment of particular difficulty, it was an act of criminal folly."

Thereupon the Battersea M.P. was removed to the cells.

Electric Supply.

Walthamstow Municipal electricity undertaking are discontinuing their supply to all trades except those connected with the food supply—including breweries.

Postponements.

Among the functions which have been postponed are the following : The Salvation Army Festival which was to have been presided over by Sir Thomas Inskip, the Solicitor-General, on Saturday, May 8th, at the Central Hall, Westminster ; the British Ladies' Golf Championship arranged to be played at Harlech next week ; the Annual Conference of the Licensed Victuallers' Defence League at Scarborough. The City of London School announce that they will open on Monday next. The National Road Walking Championship which was to have been held at St. Albans on Saturday next has been postponed.

Printed for and Published by The London Daily Express, Workers Printers, London, E.W.I.

An emergency edition of the *Daily Express*, produced during the General Strike of 1926.

---

the *Daily Express*. In 1940 he returned to politics, at the request of his close friend, Winston Churchill, and served as Minister of Aircraft Production (1940-41), Minister of Supply (1941-42) and Lord Privy Seal (1943-45). He was also entrusted with a key role in organizing Anglo-American aid to Russia.

Beaverbrook was on close terms with many powerful men and loved political intrigue. A passionate supporter of the British Empire, he consistently tried to use his newspapers to convert the British public to his views; there is little evidence that he had much lasting influence on popular attitudes. Himself a man of boundless energy, Beaverbrook once said of Lloyd George that "he did not care in which direction the car was travelling so long as he remained in the driver's seat". Much the same might have been said of Beaverbrook himself.

> "He is a magnet to all young men, and I warn you if you talk to him no good will come of it." (Clement Attlee to junior Labour ministers, 1945)
>
> ---
>
> "If Max gets to Heaven he won't last long. He will be chucked out for trying to pull off a merger between Heaven and Hell . . . after having secured a controlling interest in key subsidiary companies in both places, of course." (H. G. Wells)
>
> ---
>
> "This is my final word. It is time for me to become an apprentice once more. I have not settled in which direction. But somewhere, sometime, soon." (Beaverbrook's last public statement, May 1964)

1916 he helped to overthrow Asquith as Prime Minister in favour of Lloyd George. A month later the new Prime Minister recognized the value of his support and he was created a peer. In 1918 he became Minister of Information and Chancellor of the Duchy of Lancaster. Lloyd George could nevertheless say of his friend: ". . . he likes me and I like him, but that would not prevent him doing me in".

When the war ended, Beaverbrook devoted his great energies to building up a newspaper empire, his most important publication being

BENTHAM,
Jeremy
(1748–1832)

The founder of the "Utilitarian" school of philosophy was a child prodigy who grew up to be an enfant terrible. Admitted to Queen's College, Oxford at 12, Bentham became both a lawyer and a critic of the law. Outraged by inefficiency, corruption and injustice, he yet maintained a cool and analytical approach to

Jeremy Bentham, portrait by Henry William Pickersgill, 1829.

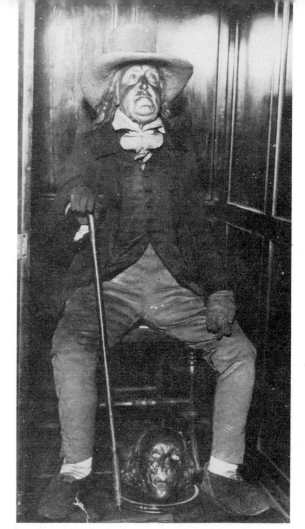

At University College, London, Bentham's mummified head rests below an effigy of him, dressed in his own clothes.

the problem of making law appropriate to a rapidly changing society. In an age when most thinkers venerated laws as an expression of the wisdom of past generations, Bentham constantly called them into question by asking very simply "what use are they?", hence the name "Utilitarianism" for his style of thinking. Bentham's "measure of right and wrong" was that any law or institution should tend to promote "the greatest happiness of the greatest number".

His own practical efforts at reform were few, but significant. He planned a new sort of prison, the Panopticon, in which the inmates would be kept under constant surveillance and taught to "love labour" by doing useful work. He also helped to found University

College, London as an institution of higher education open to students of any religion. And he made many practical suggestions for other useful reforms — the registration of births, deaths and marriages, the taking of a regular census of population and even the cutting of canals at Suez and Panama. His most important contribution, however, was to make reform respectable at a time when the fear induced by the French Revolution threatened to brand any criticism of existing institutions as tantamount to treason.

Bentham's influence stretched far beyond England and affected the development of societies as far apart as Russia and Latin America. Unfortunately, such disciples as Edwin Chadwick retained Bentham's passion for efficiency but lost sight of his concern for humanity.

> "He meditates the coming age. He hears and sees only what suits his purpose . . . and looks out for facts and passing occurrences in order to put them into his logical machinery and grind them into the dust and powder of some subtle theory . . . ." (William Hazlitt, 1778-1830)

> "The arch-philistine Jeremy Bentham was the insipid, pedantic, leather-tongued oracle of the bourgeois intelligence of the nineteenth century." (Karl Marx, *Das Kapital*)

> ". . . he is the great *subversive*, or in the language of continental philosophers, the great *critical*, thinker of his age and country." (John Stuart Mill)

BEVAN,
Aneurin
(1897-1960)

A left-wing socialist and a first-class orator, "Nye" Bevan was adored and hated but never ignored. A miner's son, he left school at 13 and worked at the coal face, then rose rapidly through his union to become spokesman for

The Labour Left, 1951 — Harold Wilson, Aneurin Bevan, Ian Mikardo, Tom Driberg, Barbara Castle.

Child welfare foods also became available free through the NHS. Harold Hill Health Centre, 1963.

the miners of South Wales in the 1926 General Strike. In 1929 he was elected MP for Ebbw Vale, and made his mark in Parliament as one of Churchill's most effective critics during the Second World War. As Minister of Health (1945-51), he conducted the complex negotiations with the doctors' organizations which led to the establishment of the National Health Service, his one great legislative achievement. He resigned as Minister of Labour (1951) in protest against the introduction of health-service charges to meet higher defence spending, and continued to criticize this policy until 1957 when, as chief Labour spokesman on foreign affairs, he opposed his former followers who demanded that Britain give up nuclear arms. Bevan was elected Deputy Leader of the Labour Party in 1959, but died shortly afterwards. He was a man of great personal charm and uncertain temper, with a splendid gift for the striking phrase. He was the darling of the Left and of the constituencies and as greatly loved by ordinary party members as he was heartily disliked by Conservatives who feared his tongue as much as they disapproved of his views.

"The language of priorities is the religion of Socialism." (Aneurin Bevan)

"We know what happens to people who stay in the middle of the road. They get run over." (Aneurin Bevan)

"He enjoys prophesying the imminent fall of the capitalist system, and is prepared to play a part, any part, in its burial, except that of mute." (Harold Macmillan, 1934)

BEVERIDGE,
Lord (William Henry Beveridge)
(1879-1963)

If any one man can be called the architect of Britain's welfare state, that man was William Beveridge. Social work in London's East End led him to study poverty and its causes and in 1909 to publish his conclusions in a work called *Unemployment : a problem of Industry*. Winston Churchill, then President of the Board of Trade, invited him to supervise the establishment of a system of "labour exchanges",

which would help men find work, and to work out a practical plan for compulsory unemployment insurance, to ensure that they had some income when they could not work. From 1909 to 1916 Beveridge worked as Director of Labour Exchanges and from 1919 to 1937 as Director of the London School of Economics, where he encouraged the practical study of real-life social problems.

In 1941 Beveridge was asked to head an enquiry into the working of the existing system of social insurance. The Report he presented in 1942 was expected to be merely a technical document, recommending certain minor reforms in the interests of greater efficiency; but it went much further than this

The cartoon was captioned "RIGHT TURN".

Lord Beveridge, 1962.

and sketched out a scheme for a comprehensive system of social security "from the cradle to the grave". The Beveridge Report insisted that benefits should be payable to all, without the hated "means test" of the depression years, that there should be a system of "family allowances" to bring up the income levels of large families, and that governments should assume responsibility for maintaining full employment. The major recommendations of the Report became law under the Labour government of 1945-50. The Beveridge Report asserted that "the object of government in peace and in war is not the glory of rulers or races but the happiness of the common man"; and it gave practical effect to that belief.

BEVIN,
Ernest
(1881–1951)

Born in poverty in Somerset, Bevin first worked as a farm labourer, before becoming a carter in Bristol, working with dockers. In 1911 he became Assistant Secretary of the Dockers' Union. Ten years later he was able to unite some forty unions to form the Transport and General Workers' Union, the largest single union in the world. A prominent member of the TUC General Council (Chairman in 1937), Bevin showed great skill in settling disputes between different unions. He was also greatly interested in international affairs and travelled widely in the years between the wars.

"Our Ernie" — dockers' leader.

Bevin, by Sir David Low, 1933.

In 1940 Bevin joined Churchill's Coalition as Minister of Labour, though he was not yet an MP, with responsibility for mobilizing the nation's workers for war. In 1945 he became Foreign Secretary in Attlee's Labour Government, a post he held until a few weeks before his death. His main achievements were the creation of NATO (1949), which has remained the cornerstone of Britain's defence policy ever since, and the formulation of the Colombo Plan, which marked the beginning of development aid programmes between the industrialized nations and the developing world. He was unable, however, to find any magic answer to the problems of troubled Palestine, which Britain evacuated in 1948. Popular with many Conservatives for his hostility to Communism — one described him as "a diamond lying on a heap of coke" — Bevin was often disliked by left-wing members of his own party.

BOOTH,
Charles
(1840-1916)

A Liverpool merchant and shipowner, Charles Booth was both a wealthy man and a clever one. He became interested in social issues during the election campaign of 1865, while working for the Liberals in one of the poorest districts of his native city. As an agnostic, Booth rejected religious explanations of poverty as an inevitable consequence of human sin or part of the God-given order of society. Instead, he looked for an answer by using the methods of the new science of

Charles Booth.

sociology to make a detailed survey of the incomes and living standards of the people of London. The seventeen volumes of *The Life and Labour of the People of London* (1887-1903) amassed a vast amount of detailed information about incomes, occupations, diets and household spending and showed clearly how each was related to the others. Booth broke new ground by producing an objective definition of poverty — not having enough income to maintain physical efficiency. And he proved that one third of the population of the capital of the world's greatest empire fell below that standard. But Booth did more than simply measure poverty. His attempt "to show the numerical relation which poverty, misery and depravity bear to regular earnings" was so successful that it became difficult to hold the traditional view that poverty, vice and crime were caused by individual failings of character rather than by economic circumstances. Thus Booth's work not only provided abundant evidence of the need for better welfare services, but also challenged the beliefs which had for so long held back their development.

BOOTH,
William ("General Booth")
(1829–1912)

The founder of the Salvation Army was a Methodist preacher before he established an Evangelical mission in London's East End in 1865. He began with preaching, all-night prayer sessions and soup kitchens for the destitute. The Salvation Army, with its

"General Booth" and representatives of his "soldiers" from all parts of the world, 1907.

A lodging house, St Giles's, London — the kind of poverty which Booth studied and wrote about.

A Salvation Army soup kitchen, December 1930.

BRIGHT,
John
(1811-89)

John Bright was the liberal conscience of Victorian England. The son of a wealthy Quaker manufacturer, Bright was, as leader of the Anti-Corn Law League (1839-46), a forthright supporter of Free Trade and an outspoken critic of the landowning classes and their traditional political power. As a

John Bright signed this drawing of himself by Frederick Sargent.

military ranks, uniforms and bands, was established in 1878. Booth's book about the wretched conditions of the "submerged tenth", the poorest of the poor — *In Darkest England and the Way Out* — exposed the appalling housing conditions of the slum areas and called for a programme of colonization to give slum-dwellers a chance to make a decent life for themselves. It also brought in a public subscription of £100,000 to further his charitable work.

Booth saw himself as conducting a holy war against sin and the Devil. Low wages and the exploitation of women were particular targets of his, and he spoke out without restraint against the social injustice he saw around him. As he put it in his own words, "I like my tea as I like my religion — hot!"

In 1880 the first Salvation Army missions were established in the United States and the following year in Australia. By the time of Booth's death the Army was active in fifty-nine countries, relieving the outcast in areas avoided by other charities and proclaiming the gospel through words and music in a way that was simple, straightforward and self-confident. Through his creation, the Salvation Army, Booth ensured that his life was not merely a protest but a successful one.

DR. BRIGHT AND HIS PATIENT.

Doctor. *"Do you get good wages?"*
Patient. *"Yes."*
Doctor. *"Have you plenty to eat and drink?"*
Patient. *"Yes, as far as that goes."*
Doctor. *"Do you do as you like?"*
Patient. *"Yes."*
Doctor. *"Do you pay taxes?"*
Patient. *"Now to knock me over!"*
Doctor. *"Ah! We must change all that. We want you for REFORM!"*

☞ This colloquy gives a not unfair summary of Mr. Bright's address to his constituents in the preceding month.—1865.

BROWN,
Lancelot ("Capability")
(1716-83)

Capability Brown has left a mark on the English landscape which has lasted to this day. "I see great capability of improvement here," he would tell his aristocratic patrons. But the improvements that he made were often immensely costly in terms of money and labour. On one estate he caused 100,000 new trees to be planted. At Milton Abbas he moved an entire village half a mile because it spoiled a view.

Brown's carefully planted clumps of trees, his winding paths and picturesque ruins were artfully arranged to resemble a "natural" landscape, a landscape which conveniently came right up to the great house from whose

"Capability" Brown, engraving after a portrait of c. 1770.

Member of Parliament (1843-89), he was a fearless champion of unpopular causes, criticizing the Crimean War and abuses of British power in Ireland and India and supporting the abolition of capital punishment and the admission of Jews to Parliament. Bright also took a leading part in establishing the Liberal Party, and helped to initiate the campaign to grant the vote to all householders. In 1868 he joined Gladstone's first Ministry, but resigned in 1870 on grounds of ill-health. He served again under Gladstone in 1873-74 and 1880-82 before resigning in protest against the bombardment of Alexandria. In his later years Bright's views became more conservative and he opposed trade unionism, women's rights and Home Rule for Ireland.

windows it could be surveyed to best advantage. The writer Horace Walpole observed that "so clearly did he copy nature that his works would be mistaken for it". But it should not be forgotten that, in creating his masterpieces, Capability Brown, who had little use for flowers or the geometrically ordered shrubs so beloved of previous generations, destroyed some fine formal gardens.

Brown's ideas of natural beauty influenced not only other landscape gardeners but also generations of architects, painters and poets. Much of his work survives, the most famous examples being the grounds of Blenheim Palace, Oxfordshire and Kew Gardens in London.

In the gardens at Blenheim Palace.

BRUNEL,
Isambard Kingdom
(1806-59)

The son of an eminent French engineer, Sir Marc Isambard Brunel (1769-1849), Isambard Kingdom Brunel was educated at the Lycée Henri IV in Paris and in the London engineering workshops of Thomas Maudslay. Brunel's first major project was to assist his father in building the Rotherhithe tunnel under the Thames. As chief engineer of the Great Western Railway, he then designed the entire lay-out from London, Paddington to Bristol, Temple

Clifton Suspension Bridge.

Meads. Interest in marine engineering led him to construct the *Great Western*, the second steamship to cross the Atlantic, the *Great Britain*, the first all-iron steamship, and the costly and disastrous *Great Eastern*, at the time of its construction the largest ship ever built. Among his other projects were the Royal Albert Bridge across the river Tamar and the Clifton suspension bridge across the Avon gorge at Bristol. Daniel Gooch, the engineer and Brunel's closest friend, said of him that "by his death the greatest of England's engineers was lost. . . .The commercial world thought him extravagant; but although he was so, things are not done by those who sit down and count the cost of every thought and act". Versatile and dynamic, Brunel was a restless genius whose achievements matched his reputation but whose good fortune did not.

Brunel, standing before the chains of the *Great Eastern* — a photograph of 1857.

"I suppose a sort of middle path will be the most likely — a mediocre success — an engineer sometimes employed, sometimes not — £200 or £300 and that uncertain." (Brunel on himself, 1828)

"Everything has prospered, everything at this moment is sunshine. I don't like it — it can't last . . . ." (Brunel on himself, 1835)

BURDETT-COUTTS,
Angela, Baroness
(1814–1906)

Baroness Burdett-Coutts, a miniature painted by Sir William Charles Ross, c. 1847.

The daughter of Sir Francis Burdett, an aristocratic radical politician, and the grand-daughter of Thomas Coutts the banker, Angela Burdett-Coutts became "the richest heiress in all England" at the age of 23. For the next sixty years she entertained countless British and foreign celebrities, busied herself with literally hundreds of charitable projects and took an active interest in her family's banking business. Her generosity to the Church of England resulted in the building of numerous churches and the establishment of the bishoprics of Cape Town, Adelaide and British Columbia. Her interest in education led to the introduction of cooking and sewing as part of the curriculum in elementary schools and, at the other end of the academic spectrum, to the development of the study of geology at Oxford. She also subsidized the Ragged

School Union and training ships for poor boys and helped to found the National Society for the Prevention of Cruelty to Children. She took a keen interest in the conditions of London's poor and Ireland's peasantry, pioneering model housing and youth clubs for the former and assisting emigration to the colonies for the latter. Her love of animals made her the natural leader of the Royal Society for the Prevention of Cruelty to Animals. Created baroness in 1871, she married at last in 1881 and, upon her death, was buried in Westminster Abbey.

Columbia Market, Bethnal Green, 1869 — now demolished. It was built by Miss Burdett-Coutts so that the poor of London's East End could buy fresh vegetables cheaply.

BURKE,
Edmund
(1727-97)

Edmund Burke is often regarded as the founder of modern British Conservatism, though most of his political career was passed in the service of the Whig Party. The main emphasis of his philosophy was a distrust of abstract reasoning about man and society. Instead, he placed his faith in the necessity of gradual change based on practical experience. Most of his writings were prompted by the actual events in which he was involved.

Born the son of an Irish lawyer and educated at Trinity College, Dublin, Burke first made his reputation as a writer, being a friend of

Edmund Burke, portrait by Sir Joshua Reynolds, 1771.

A cartoon of May 1791, showing Sheridan, Burke and Fox.

The IMPEACHMENT,___ or ___"The Father of the Gang, turn'd King's Evidence.

Dr Samuel Johnson. He also founded the famous and still published *Annual Register*, a chronicle of public events. He entered politics as Private Secretary to the Whig Prime Minister, Lord Rockingham, in 1765 and in his early years defended John Wilkes, criticized royal attempts to control Parliament and urged the government to compromise with the rebel American colonies. Burke took a leading part in the trial of Warren Hastings (1732-1818), arguing forcefully that British rule in India involved the obligation to govern for the benefit of its inhabitants, and not merely for Britain's own advantage. In 1790 his most famous work, *Reflections on the Revolution in France*, warned that the crisis in French politics would lead to widespread violence and the creation of a military dictatorship. Burke's emphatic attack on revolutionary change was reinforced by his desertion to the Tory Party in 1792. If his beliefs can be summarized in a sentence, it is that "Good order is the foundation of all things".

Dr Johnson said of him:

You could not stand five minutes with that man beneath a shed, while it rained, but you must be convinced you had been standing with the greatest man you had ever seen.

BYRON,
George Gordon, Lord
(1788-1824)

Poet, lover, traveller and outcast, Byron is identified in the popular imagination with the heroes he created, who were likewise poets, lovers, travellers and outcasts. From his family Byron inherited a title, a decayed estate and a tradition of drink and debauchery. Born with a crippled foot, of which he was acutely conscious, he grew into an athletic and handsome young man. He was educated at Harrow and Cambridge, and published his first book of poems *Hours of Idleness* while still an

Byron in Albanian costume, engraved after a painting by Thomas Phillips, 1813.

undergraduate. Stung by the unfavourable notices this volume received, he replied with a cutting verse satire called "English Bards and Scotch Reviewers". After a two-year tour of Greece and the Mediterranean, Byron published his first major work, *Childe Harold*, in 1812. It was an immediate sensation. In Byron's own words, "I awoke one morning and found myself famous". A series of romantic narrative poems followed in rapid succession, each enjoying extravagant popular success. *The Corsair* is said to have sold 14,000 copies in a single day.

Byron was the toast of fashionable men and the favourite of fashionable women. Then he married the cold, clever, rich Ann Milbanke. A daughter was born to them but within a year the couple parted, Ann hinting that her husband had an immoral relationship with his half-sister, Augusta. Byron became a target for open insult and left England for good. The first years of Byron's exile were spent in Venice, where he wrote his masterpiece *Don Juan*. He found an appropriate death at Missolonghi, fighting for the cause of Greek independence from Turkish rule. For the Greeks he remains a national hero, for Europeans the type of the romantic genius.

The writer Hazlitt described him as "the spoiled child of fame as well as fortune". And Byron wrote of himself:

There are but two sentiments to which I am constant — a strong love of liberty and a detestation of cant, and neither is calculated to gain me friends.

"He is the absolute monarch of words and uses them, as Bonaparte did lives, for conquest, without more regard to their intrinsic value." (Lady Byron)

". . . except for his genius, he was an ordinary nineteenth century English gentleman, with little culture and no ideas." (Matthew Arnold)

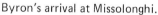
Byron's arrival at Missolonghi.

CHADWICK,
Sir Edwin
(1800–90)

Chadwick was one of the first of the "techno-crats", a firm believer in the use of science and state power to tackle the problems of society. A disciple of the reforming philo-sopher Jeremy Bentham, Edwin Chadwick was closely involved in the improvement of factory conditions (1833) and the reorgani-zation of the poor relief system (1834); but he is best remembered for his work as a

Edwin Chadwick, marble bust by Adam Salomon, c. 1863.

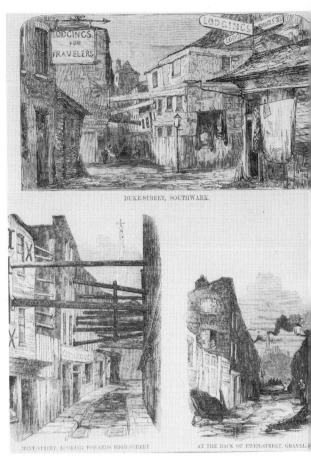

DUKE-STREET, SOUTHWARK.

MINT-STREET, LOOKING TOWARDS HIGH-STREET.   AT THE BACK OF EWER-STREET, GRAVEL L

Street scenes of 1853.

pioneer of modern public health measures. His famous *Report on the Sanitary Condition of the Labouring Population* (1842) revealed that "the annual slaughter in England and Wales from preventible cases of typhus which attacks persons in the vigour of life, appears to be double the amount of what was suffered by the Allied Armies in the battle of Waterloo." Chadwick argued that public expenditure on pure water supplies and refuse disposal systems would lead to dramatic reductions in deaths from infectious diseases. As an expert member of the Board of Health (1848-54), Chadwick promoted the cause of "sanitary reform" with more vigour than tact, making many political enemies. He was not knighted until 1889, when the importance of his contri-bution to social administration was at last recognized.

CHAMBERLAIN,
Joseph
(1836-1914)

AN EXPLORATORY OPERATION

THE BUTCHER: You needn't be alarmed; I am only going to perform a slight exploratory operation—just for the sake of inquiry.

THE GOOSE THAT LAYS THE GOLDEN EGGS: Murder!

A cartoon from a collection of *Political Caricatures* published in 1903-4.

Having made his fortune in industry, Chamberlain, as Lord Mayor of Birmingham, won a national reputation with his imaginative "Corporation St." slum clearance scheme. Entering Parliament in 1876, he helped to reorganize the Liberal Party and served as President of the Board of Trade under Gladstone (1880-85), until his opposition to Home Rule for Ireland split the government and led to its fall in 1886. Moving over to the Conservatives, Chamberlain served as Colonial Secretary (1895-1903), supporting British expansion in Africa and trying to promote the idea of an imperial federation. He also established schools of tropical medicine in London

Joe Chamberlain offers a Birmingham audience a "Free Trade" loaf and a "Protectionist" loaf and defies them to tell the difference, 1904.

and Liverpool and played a large part in the peace settlement which ended the Boer War. Believing that "Empire is Commerce", Chamberlain then turned to the cause of "Tariff Reform" and argued for a system of trade barriers which would discriminate in favour of goods produced within the British Empire. This attack on the established policy of Free Trade divided the Conservative Party, as Home Rule had the Liberals, and contributed to its defeat at the election of 1906. In the same year this most controversial of politicians was struck down by paralysis, which kept him out of politics until his death.

Disraeli said that he "looked and spoke like a cheesemonger" and Asquith said he had "the manners of a cad and the tongue of a bargee". But Gladstone observed that he was "expecting to play an historical part and probably destined to it". And Churchill called him "incomparably the most live, sparkling, insurgent, compulsive figure in British affairs".

37

CHAMBERLAIN,
(Arthur) Neville
(1869-1940)

Peace in our time? Neville Chamberlain displays his Munich agreement with Hitler, Heston airport, 30 September 1938.

To most people, Neville Chamberlain's name means "Munich" and a foolish claim to have secured "peace for our time" by weakly betraying Czechoslovakia to Hitler. But Chamberlain's political career shows him to have been neither a weak man nor a foolish one. The son of Joseph Chamberlain, he followed his father's example by becoming a successful businessman and serving twice as

Neville Chamberlain, 1924, leaving Buckingham Palace, where the new government ministers had been presented with their seals.

Mayor of Birmingham. Entering Parliament as a Conservative in 1918, he won rapid promotion, thanks to his mastery of adminis-tration, and was responsible for important reforms in local government, health, housing and the relief of poverty. In opposition (1920-31), he reorganized the Conservative Party and, as Chancellor of the Exchequer (1931-37), reintroduced protection and tried to revive industry in depressed areas. His brisk and business-like manner helped him get things done and made him Baldwin's right-hand man, but did not make him popular. As Prime Minister (1937-40), Chamberlain was forced into the unfamiliar field of foreign affairs at a time of grave international crisis. A dying man when war broke out, he made an unconvincing national leader and resigned to make way for Churchill in April 1940. Characteristically, he continued to serve as a loyal and hard-working member of the Cabinet until shortly before his death. He deserves to be remembered as a most able if unlucky politician.

CHAPLIN,
Charlie (Sir Charles)
(1889–1977)

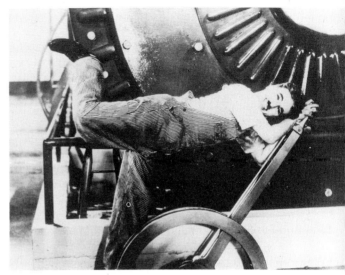

Charlie Chaplin in *Modern Times*.

Charlie Chaplin was the cinema's first international super-star. Born in a London slum, the son of an alcoholic music-hall artist, he first appeared on stage at the age of five. In 1913, touring America with the famous Fred Karno variety troupe, Chaplin was invited to join Mack Sennett's successful Keystone film studio at a salary of $150 a week. Here he made 35 silent slapstick comedies, rapidly developing the character of the tramp, which was to make him world-famous. The tramp, shabby but gallant, oppressed but resourceful, seemed to appeal to all ages and classes. By

Charlie Chaplin with Jackie Coogan, "The Kid".

1918 Chaplin had been signed up by First National Studios to make eight films for $100,000. In the following year he joined Mary Pickford, Douglas Fairbanks and D. W. Griffith to form the United Artists corporation to encourage independent film-making. By 1920, when Chaplin made his classic comedy *The Kid*, he had become the subject of songs and souvenirs. When he visited Europe in 1921 he was greeted by wildly cheering crowds of fans. *The Gold Rush* (1925) and *City Lights* (1931) sustained his popularity but, with the onset of the world depression, Chaplin began to use his comedy to highlight contemporary problems. In *Modern Times* (1936) he dealt with the boredom of factory life and in *The Great Dictator* (1940), the first film in which he actually spoke, he presented a brilliant caricature of Hitler and the threat of Nazism. Chaplin's sympathy for radical causes and his war-time support for Russia led to his being branded a Communist. He left America to settle in Switzerland in 1952. He returned from exile to receive an Oscar in 1972 and was knighted in 1975. A brilliant gymnast, an inspired mime, a gifted composer and a superbly professional film-maker, Chaplin used his many talents to champion the rights of the "little man". The little man, in his millions, recognized this with his laughter and his applause.

CHURCHILL,
Sir Winston Leonard Spencer
(1874-1965)

The son of a brilliant and wayward politician, Lord Randolph Churchill, and a beautiful American heiress, Jennie Jerome, Winston Churchill was born in Blenheim Palace, the grandson of the Seventh Duke of Marlborough. He was educated at Harrow and Sandhurst and was originally destined for a military career. Commissioned into the cavalry, he soon became a war correspondent and saw action in Cuba, on the North-West Frontier of India, in the Sudan, where he joined in the charge at the battle of Omdurman (1898), and in the Boer War, where he was captured and escaped single-handed, becoming a

The Warlord — Churchill with his generals and Eden (far left), Eisenhower (second right) and Montgomery (far right).

national hero. Elected as a Conservative MP in 1900, Churchill joined the Liberals in 1904 and became President of the Board of Trade in succession to his friend, Lloyd George. As Home Secretary (1910-11), he was involved in the controversial Tonypandy miners' dispute in Wales and in the "Siege of Sidney Street" in London's East End. These incidents, and his belligerent attitude during the General Strike of 1926, earned him a reputation as an enemy of the working classes, which his genuine interest in social reforms belied. Churchill's first three constituencies were all in poor industrial areas, and he worked hard to assist his constituents with their problems at a time when few Members saw this as an important part of their duties. He also introduced such important measures as the establishment of labour exchanges and the regulation of wages in the small-workshop "sweated industries".

As First Lord of the Admiralty (1911-1915), Churchill supported the modernization of the navy, the development of aviation and the improvement of sailors' living conditions. It

1946 — Redundant Hero.

was largely due to his foresight that the navy was fully mobilized when war broke out in 1914. In 1915 Churchill, who had made many political enemies in his rapid rise, was made the chief scapegoat for the disastrous failure of the Gallipoli landings — although the naval aspect of the operation, which was his sole personal responsibility, was entirely successful. Rejoining the army he commanded a battalion of the Royal Scots Fusiliers on the Western Front until May 1916, when Lloyd George restored him to office as Minister of Munitions (1917-18). He then served as Minister for War and Air (1919-20) and as Colonial Secretary (1921-22), supervising the demobilization of the armed forces and the enforcement of the post-war peace settlement in the Middle East.

Losing his seat in 1922, Churchill left the Liberals and was elected as a "constitutional anti-socialist" in 1924. Baldwin invited him to become Chancellor of the Exchequer (1924-29), and he re-joined the Conservatives in 1925. From 1929 to 1939 his opposition to

Indian nationalism and his criticisms of the reassertion of German national power kept him out of office and he seriously considered retiring from politics for good. But the outbreak of war saw him return to office as First Lord of the Admiralty.

In May 1940 Churchill became Prime Minister of a Coalition Government, Labour refusing to serve under any other leader. His inspiring speeches in the Commons and to the nation led President John F. Kennedy to say of him later that "he mobilized the English language and sent it into battle". Tireless, in spite of severe health problems, Churchill conducted a personal diplomacy with Roosevelt and Stalin and provided a constant stimulus both to his generals and to the public at large. His main aims were to hold together the anti-Nazi coalition at all costs and to communicate to the British people, their allies and the oppressed peoples of occupied Europe his unshakable faith in ultimate victory. In these he succeeded.

Defeated at the General Election of 1945, Churchill warned in a memorable speech at Fulton, Missouri, that an "iron curtain" was descending across Europe. In his final term as Prime Minister (1951-55) he was preoccupied with ensuring that the Cold War between Russia and the West should not escalate into a nuclear holocaust.

In his later years Churchill was showered with honours. In 1953 he was awarded the Nobel Prize for Literature and made a Knight of the Garter, declining any higher title. In 1963 the United States Congress conferred upon him the status of Honorary Citizen of the United States, a unique distinction. Soldier, politician, journalist, lecturer, historian and painter, he was, in the words of the *Times* obituary, "the greatest Englishman of his time".

> "He is a young man who will go far if he doesn't overbalance!" (Cecil Rhodes)
>
> "a good judge in every matter which does not concern himself." (Lord Beaverbrook)
>
> "He has spoilt himself by reading about Napoleon." (Lloyd George)

COBBETT,
William
(1763-1835)

Soldier, farmer and journalist, Radical and Conservative, living at the time of England's great transition from agriculture to industry, Cobbett chronicled and commented upon practically every subject from high politics to the price of potatoes. Having soldiered in Canada (1784-91) and visited revolutionary France, he emigrated to the newly-independent United States (1793-1800), where he

William Cobbett, the *Register*.

The Amusing Chronicle. d   Repository for Miscellaneous Literature.

William Cobbett Esq.

Continues to be Published regularly every Saturday, at No. 6, Gilberts Passage, Portugal Street. Price Four Pence.

Cobbett's accounts of his journeys through the changing and troubled English countryside, published in book form as *Rural Rides* (1830), are the best known of his more than forty published works, but his personal favourite was his *Poor Man's Friend* (1826), "a Defence of the Rights of those who do the Work and fight the Battles". A life-long opponent of corruption and injustice, Cobbett was a man of strong prejudices and affections, a hater of money-lenders, railways and tea-drinking and a champion of the farm labourer and self-employed craftsman. As a practical crusader, Cobbett was not a success, although in Parliament he did make fine speeches in support of factory reform and against the new Poor Law. His real significance lies not in what he did but in what he was — a fearless and romantic John Bull, embattled against the soulless, money-grubbing city life that was overwhelming the old England he idealized. He was distinguished for his energy and his style rather than his consistency. As John Stuart Mill was to write of him:

There were two sorts of people he could not endure, those who differed from him and those who agreed with him.

Cobbett, portrayed by Gillray, 1809.

wrote political pamphlets against the French and Tom Paine until a heavy fine for libel drove him back to England. Here his weekly *Political Register* attacked paper money and the growth of London ("the great Wen") and called for the reform of Parliament. Cobbett's outspoken criticism of flogging in the army earned him two years in prison but, unrepentant, he came out to found a cheaper version of the *Register*, which sold 40,000 copies a week and was thus one of the most influential journals of its day. Fleeing once more to the United States, for fear of arrest, he farmed on Long Island (1817-19) before returning home, with the bones of his former opponent, Tom Paine, to denounce government restrictions on civil liberties (the Six Acts) and to support the cause of Catholic Emancipation. In 1832, after two unsuccessful attempts, Cobbett was finally elected to Parliament.

"It is not true that he belonged successively to two parties . . . . The truth is that the confusion was not in Cobbett but in the terms Tory and Radical. They are not exact terms; they are nothing like so exact as Cobbett was." (G. K. Chesterton)

"He was honest; he never saw more than one side of a subject at a time." (Daniel O'Connell)

CONSTABLE,
John
(1776–1837)

John Constable is probably one of the few painters whose work is instantly recognizable to the average Englishman. Reproductions of *The Haywain* (1820) now hang in hundreds of thousands of homes, yet in his day Constable's talent brought him only a late and modest success. The son of a Suffolk miller, he trained at the Royal Academy but, unlike Turner, only gradually won recognition in England. Constable's genius lay in the portrayal of nature, as his French contemporaries, Gericault and Delacroix, realized. His view of nature was clearly expressed in his statement that "I never saw an ugly thing in my life. Neither were there ever two leaves of a tree alike since the creation of the world." After his death Constable had no true successor, though many imitators.

John Constable, portrait by Ramsay Richard Reinagle, c. 1798.

The Haywain — Constable's best-known painting.

COOK,
Captain James
(1728-79)

Cook's map of New Zealand, published 1772.

Born the son of a Yorkshire farm labourer and apprenticed to a Whitby coal-shipper, Cook joined the navy as an ordinary seaman in 1755 and within two years was given his own command. His skill in making a hydrographic survey of the St Lawrence river led to his being commissioned to map the coast of Newfoundland (1763-68) and, in 1769, he was chosen to lead an expedition to the South Pacific. This voyage had two major aims — to observe the transit of Venus, an event which

Captain Cook, portrait by Sir Nathaniel Dance, 1776, painted for Sir Joseph Banks.

would make it possible to achieve a precise measurement of the distance between the earth and the sun; and to forestall any possible French attempts to colonize the area, by discovering and claiming territories first. In the course of the three-year voyage Cook not only made the necessary observations but also showed that, if an undiscovered "southern continent" existed, it was much smaller than had generally been supposed, and also that New Zealand consisted of two separate islands. In the course of a second voyage (1772-75) Cook sailed right round the world, became the first navigator to cross the Antarctic Circle and, by insisting that his crew ate plenty of fresh fruit and vegetables, ended the seaman's curse of scurvy. Indeed, not a single man died during this voyage, an unprecedented achievement. Cook's last expedition was intended to find a northern sea passage between the Pacific and the Atlantic, but adverse weather forced him south to Hawaii, where, after a tragic misunderstanding, he was killed by the local people. No single man added more to European knowledge of the world.

COOK,
Thomas
(1808-92)

The inventor of modern tourism left school at 10 and became a Baptist missionary at 28. A zealous supporter of the crusade against drink, he organized the first ever public railway excursion in 1841, taking 500 people from Leicester to Loughborough to attend a temperance meeting. In 1855 Cook conducted groups from Leicester to Calais, to enable them to visit the Paris Exhibition. In 1856 he led his first guided tour of Europe. By the following decade, the business of Thos. Cook and Son had expanded so much that he gave up leading tours personally and became a full-time agent for the sale of travel tickets. By the 1880s the firm was arranging military transport and postal services for the Government and organizing guided tours of areas as distant as the Middle East.

A page from Cook's brochure, 1903.

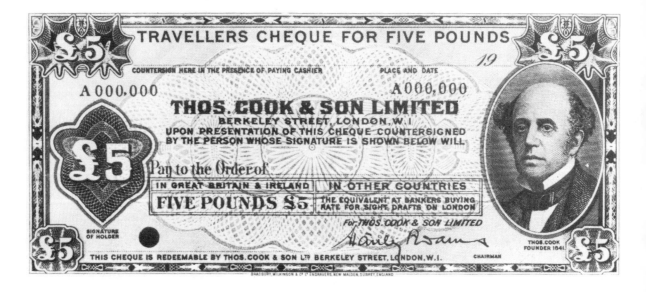

COWARD,
Sir Noel
(1899-1973)

Noel Coward was a theatrical genius in every sense of the word. As a singer and dancer he was more than competent; as an actor (from the age of 12) he had few equals; as a playwright and director no rivals in his time. His plays (*Private Lives*, 1930; *Blithe Spirit*, 1941) and songs ("Mad Dogs and Englishmen"; "I'll See You Again") were light and witty and sometimes more profound than at first they seemed. Although he lived most of his later life abroad, Coward's attachment to England was very strong, as his historical pageant, *Cavalcade* (1931), and his war-time tribute to the Royal Navy, *In Which We Serve*, clearly show.

Making-up for the part of King Magnus in Shaw's *The Apple Cart*.

Composer composed.

CURZON,
Lord (George Nathaniel, Marquis Curzon of Kedleston) (1859-1925)

THE NEW VICEROY.
From *Fair Game.*

Lord Curzon was one of the most able politicians not to have become Prime Minister — and he often gave the impression of holding this opinion himself. Extremely clever and widely-travelled, he served as a Conservative MP (1886-98) before becoming Viceroy of India while not yet forty. An acknowledged expert on Asian affairs, he governed in India with more vigour than tact. Under Curzon, great progress was made in reforming the administration, improving agriculture and the

A photograph of 1890.

LORD CURZON AS VICEROY OF INDIA: A GROUP AT THE VICEREGAL LODGE, SIMLA
From a Photograph by Bourne and Shepherd

railways, preserving India's historic heritage and strengthening its defences. But against these achievements must be set Curzon's arrogant treatment of Indian leaders, his quarrel with Kitchener over control of the Indian army and his decision to partition the province of Bengal, which led to the first mass agitation against British rule.

As Foreign Secretary (1919-24), Curzon was largely responsible for the Treaty of Lausanne (1923), which settled the situation in the eastern Mediterranean. Passed over for the premiership, partly because he was a peer, and partly on account of his cold personality, he continued to serve in government until his death. Plagued from youth by a crippling spinal condition, Curzon was admired by many but held in affection by few. He knew that he was not popular, but failed to realize that in a democratic age this really mattered.

> "Curzon was not perhaps a great man, but he was a supreme civil servant." (Lloyd George)
>
> ---
>
> "Kipling once said to me of Curzon, that his activity was the product of bad health. Ordinary existence was barred to him. So his iron corset may have been responsible for his ill-directed drive and energy . . . ." (Lord Beaverbrook)

DARWIN,
Charles Robert
(1809–82)

Darwin's discoveries not only revolutionized scientific thinking but also had the most profound impact on the way men understood both the physical world and religion and politics as well. Yet Darwin's only systematic training in science was an 18-month period at Edinburgh University, studying to be a doctor. Darwin dropped out of the course and went

Charles Darwin, 1883. (Published in the *Century* magazine.)

A cartoon of about 1870.

to Cambridge, intending to prepare himself for the Church. However, meetings with scientists led him to accept the post of Ship's Naturalist aboard HMS *Beagle* on its world voyage of scientific exploration (1831-36). Darwin later described this adventure as "by far the most important event in my life". Aboard the *Beagle*, Darwin visited the Galapagos Islands, off the coast of Ecuador, where he discovered 14 species of finches, each distinct from one another and from any others known in the world. This discovery prompted Darwin's interest in the problem of evolution, the theory that the millions of different types of living beings in the world had not all been brought into existence by a single divine act of creation, but had gradually developed from simpler forms of life. Darwin was not the first scientist to put forward a theory of evolution, but he was the first to provide in his account of "natural selection" (suggested by his reading of Malthus' *Essay on Population*), an explanation of *how* evolution occurred, and to back his theories with detailed evidence from many different parts of the world. Basically, Darwin's argument was that no two members of the same species were *absolutely* identical, but varied slightly in size, strength, etc., and that, faced with the challenge of varying environmental conditions, those that were slightly better adapted to surviving them would do so at the expense of the rest, and pass on to their offspring the characteristics that would ensure them a better chance of survival in turn. Darwin worked painstakingly on the book which would put forward his arguments clearly and comprehensively, only to find, almost on the eve of publication, that a fellow scientist, Alfred Russell Wallace (1823-1913), had reached almost exactly the same conclusions as Darwin himself. Fortunately, the two men agreed to joint publication in the Journal of the Linnaean Society (1858). Darwin's masterpiece appeared in 1859, entitled *On the Origin of Species by Means of Natural Selection, or the Preservation of Favoured Races in the Struggle for Life*. It is usually referred to as *The Origin of Species*. Written in a clear and readable style, the book became an instant classic and the focus of furious debates in which Darwin himself took little part, though his ideas were ably defended by another scientist, T. H. Huxley (1825-95). Because Darwin's account of evolution appeared to contradict the Biblical account of the creation of the world, many men of religion denounced his work as blasphemous. Others saw in his theory of the "survival of the fittest" a justification for international rivalries, the exploitation of non-white peoples or the struggle of class against class. Darwin would have none of this "Social Darwinism", but his protests counted for little. Apart from his world-shaking *Origin of Species*, Darwin also published works of major importance on botany and geology.

> ". . . nothing can be at first sight more entirely implausible than his theory, and yet after beginning by thinking it impossible, one arrives at something like an actual belief in it . . . ." (John Stuart Mill)
>
> ". . . the more one knew of him, the more he seemed the incorporated ideal of a man of science." (T. H. Huxley)

DICKENS,
Charles John Huffam
(1812-70)

Dickens is one of the few authors who have achieved great acclaim during their own lifetime and have retained their reputation with both literary critics and the ordinary members of the reading public alike. Dickens is one of the small number of great writers whose works are not only widely read but re-read, again and again. In his works he attacked injustice

Charles Dickens with his daughters.

Oliver Twist introduced to Fagin, drawn by George Cruikshank for an 1846 edition of *Oliver Twist*.

and published, like most of his other works, in serial form (1836). Success followed success, but Dickens only worked the harder, acting as editor of his own weekly magazine, *Household Words*, as well as giving public readings from his works from 1858 until the time of his death.

Shortly before his death an American critic observed that:

No one thinks of Mr Dickens as a writer. He is at once, through his books, a friend.

"He is a very great loss. He had a large loving mind and the strongest sympathy with the poorer classes." (Queen Victoria)

"Those who dislike Dickens have an excellent case. He ought to be bad. He is actually one of our big writers . . . ." (E. M. Forster)

"Dickens's achievement was to create serious literary art out of pop material . . . ." (Anthony Burgess)

wherever he found it — in the law courts (*Bleak House*), the workhouse (*Oliver Twist*), in schools (*Nicholas Nickleby*) or in factories (*David Copperfield*). A master of descriptive writing, especially when dealing with London scenes, Dickens is perhaps best remembered as the creator of hundreds of unforgettable characters, many of whom, such as Scrooge, Fagin, Uriah Heep, and Mr Micawber, have passed into English folklore.

Dickens came from a respectable family which had fallen on hard times. When his father was imprisoned for debt, Dickens, though only a boy, was forced to live alone and work in a polish factory while his mother and the younger children accompanied his father to prison. This experience of shame and poverty distressed him greatly and may help to explain both his concern for the poor and his enjoyment of worldly success.

Dickens began his career as a reporter, first in the law courts and then in Parliament. His first published stories were short humorous articles, written under the name of "Boz". His first important novel — *The Posthumous Papers of the Pickwick Club* — was written

DISRAELI,
Benjamin (Earl of Beaconsfield)
(1804–81)

Disraeli's career represents the triumph of ambition over adversity. Born a Jew, but baptised a Christian at 12, he had little formal education and no aristocratic connections. His only assets were his intelligence and an unashamed determination "to climb to the top of the greasy pole". After several false starts as a solicitor's clerk, businessman and

Elder statesman — Lord Beaconsfield.

"MOSÉ IN EGITTO!!!"

Wily politician — *Punch* congratulates Disraeli on acquiring control of the Suez Canal.

journalist, Disraeli became an instant celebrity with the publication of his first novel *Vivien Grey* (1826), a tale of scandal in high society. In 1837, at the fifth attempt, he was elected to Parliament as a Conservative, having started out as a Radical. In 1841 he failed to gain a post in Peel's Cabinet but continued to advance his fortunes through the publication of his most famous novel, *Sybil: or The Two Nations* (1845), which showed his deep concern with the "condition-of-England question" — the problems that society was facing as a result of rapid industrialization. Disraeli argued that the gap between rich and poor, the "two nations" of the novel's sub-title, was not only economic but social and political as well and therefore a threat to the order and health of the nation as a whole. His solution was to reassert the "natural" right and duty of the landed aristocracy to provide society with the leadership it needed.

In 1846 Disraeli led the Conservative revolt

against the Party Leader, Peel, when he carried the repeal of the Corn Laws. The resulting split in the Party left Disraeli as its effective leader. Over the next twenty years, mostly in opposition, he was to establish himself as a master of debate and parliamentary tactics. These skills enabled him, in 1867, to carry the Second Reform Bill, a major constitutional reform which gave the vote to the urban working man. Disraeli served briefly as Prime Minister in 1868 and held that office continuously from 1874 to 1880. His major achievements in that period were the acquisition of control of the Suez Canal (1875), the creation of the title "Empress of India" for Queen Victoria (1877) and the avoidance of a general European war over the Eastern Question at the Congress of Berlin (1878), a diplomatic triumph which enabled him to claim that he had brought England "peace with honour" — and Cyprus as well. Disraeli's government also carried out a number of major reforms in the fields of health, housing and industrial relations, but Disraeli himself played little part in these matters, although he realized their importance.

Disraeli's witty and theatrical manner led many of his contemporaries to underestimate his significance as a thinker. Though no cold philosopher, Disraeli, in his speeches, pamphlets and novels, repeated and elaborated a number of basic themes which have been central to the Conservative outlook since his time. He denied that class conflict was inevitable and upheld the ideal of national harmony. He believed in the value of traditional institutions and was suspicious of abstract principles of reform. Above all, he was a patriot, determined to uphold British and Imperial interests abroad. These were his principles; but his opponents could never forgive him for the lack of principle with which he pursued them.

EDWARD VII
(1841-1910)

Deservedly remembered as a "prince of pleasure", Edward VII, rather less deservedly, won a reputation for being a "prince of peace"; but his part in ending the long rivalry between England and France has been exaggerated. Fluent in French and German from his early years, Edward as Prince of Wales took ill to the study and discipline prescribed for him by his serious-minded parents. His father characterised him thus:

Edward VII with the future Edward VIII, on board the Royal yacht *Victoria and Albert*, 1901.

Le Rire

A French cartoon, 2 February 1901.

and eating were among his most favoured pastimes, though he also found time for much work on behalf of charity. His love of ceremonial and lavish hospitality served him well as King (1901-10). He continued to maintain close personal contact with the crowned heads of Europe, but showed little interest in domestic politics. Edward's easy-going and pleasure-loving nature made him widely popular with rich and poor alike and his death was genuinely mourned throughout the nation. Lord Northcliffe said of him, rather cruelly, that he was "the greatest monarch we've ever had — on a racecourse." Lord Fisher was more generous: "He wasn't clever, but he always did the right thing, which is better than brains."

Sayings of Edward VII:

"We are all Socialists nowadays."

"You can tell when you have crossed into Germany because of the badness of the coffee."

"Let me introduce you to the last King of England." (On introducing Lord Haldane to the future George V.)

Bertie has remarkable social talent. He is lively, quick and sharp when his mind is set on anything, which is seldom . . . . But usually his intellect is of no more use than a pistol packed in the bottom of a trunk if one were attacked . . .

Queen Victoria believed that her son's rebellious attitude helped to drive her beloved Albert to an early grave. She therefore prevented her son from playing any serious part in public life. Unfortunately, she never ceased to think of him as a naughty boy. The Prince therefore turned his considerable energies to the task of enjoying himself. Sport, fashion, the theatre, gambling, travelling

FARADAY,
Michael
(1791–1867)

Faraday is a supreme example of the amateur tradition in English science. The son of a Yorkshire blacksmith, he was apprenticed to a London bookseller at the age of 13. In 1813 he became the Personal Assistant of the celebrated Sir Humphrey Davy at the Royal Institution and for ten years assisted his research into the chemical properties of gases. He then developed his own field of research, concentrating on the relationships between light, heat, electricity and magnetism. At 31 he read his first scientific paper before the

Michael Faraday.

Faraday's laboratory at the Royal Institution.

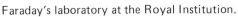

Royal Society; at 33 he was elected a Fellow. His discovery of electro-magnetic induction (1831) and diamagnetism (1845) made possible the development of electrical energy, and he can be regarded as the founder of the science of electromagnetism. Faraday not only made fundamental discoveries which form the basis of the modern electrical industry, but also invented the transformer and the dynamo and discovered benzine — and all this with only the slightest knowledge of mathematics. A brilliant experimental scientist, who seemed to work by intuition, he was also a superb lecturer and inaugurated the Royal Institution's annual Christmas lectures for young audiences.

> "He seems to have the particular talent of knowing more about what he is saying and with less pains than anybody else . . . ." (Georgiana, Duchess of Devonshire)
>
> ---
>
> ". . . he has put to hazard his ease, his security, his interest, his power, even his darling popularity, for the benefit of a people whom he has never seen. This is the road that all heroes have trod before him." (Edmund Burke)

FOX,
Charles James
(1749-1806)

Fox entered the Commons at the age of 19. He was to hold ministerial office briefly on three occasions, but it was in the House that he made his mark. For more than twenty years he was Pitt's great rival, staunchly defending the liberties of the individual and

Caricature of a Whig, published 1790. (Demosthenes was a famous Greek mob orator.)

Publish'd as the Act directs, by Bentley & C. May 1.1790.

A Demosthenean Attitude.

the press and attacking Britain's opposition to revolutionary France. Fox was idolized by many young politicians, who developed his ideas into classic nineteenth-century liberalism, with its emphasis on limiting the power of the state while increasing popular participation in the making of government policy. Personal scandal dogged Fox's career, but he made himself Pitt's equal in the Commons through sheer force of personality and his unrivalled skill as a speaker.

Charles James Fox, portrait by Karl Anton Hickel. c. 1793.

FRY, Elizabeth (1780-1845)

Born into the pious and charitable Gurney family and brought up in a loving Quaker home, Elizabeth Fry spent her life trying to help those whose lives had less secure beginnings. While still a teenager she started a school for poor children in her native Norwich. In 1813 she visited Newgate prison for the first time. Here some 300 female prisoners, with their children, lived in over-crowded squalor. From 1816 onwards Mrs

Elizabeth Fry reading to prisoners at Newgate.

Fry began to visit the prison regularly, bringing clothes and work, setting up a school for the children and running Bible classes for the women. In an age which regarded savagery and neglect as the proper response to crime, Elizabeth Fry, together with a few other reformers such as John Howard and Samuel Romilly, believed that criminals should be treated like the human beings that they still were. As she put it in her own words, "I never refer to their past; we have all sinned and come short." She pressed for separate treatment for female prisoners and the classification of prisoners according to their offences. In her later years she travelled widely in Europe in the cause of prison reform, worked to improve the treatment of the insane and the homeless and in 1840 founded the institute of Nursing Sisters in Whitechapel, to take care of poor people in their own homes. All this she accomplished despite her husband's bankruptcy (1828) and bringing up eleven children of her own.

GEORGE IV
(The Prince Regent)
(1762-1830)

As Prince of Wales, Prince Regent (1811-20) and King (1820-30), George IV aspired to be the "first gentleman of Europe", but he never even earned the respect of his own subjects. Pleasure-loving and self-indulgent, he

George IV, portrait by Sir Thomas Lawrence.

was, as a young man, at least witty, elegant and high-spirited; as an old one, he was bloated, ill-tempered and absurdly vain. Throughout his life he quarrelled with his conscientious father, George III (1738-1820), until, when the King had been finally certified as incapable of governing, he assumed the powers of Regent (1811). His attempt to divorce his estranged wife, Queen Caroline, made him widely unpopular (1820). A self-conscious leader of fashion, George IV did take a passionate, and indeed, extravagant interest in the arts, commissioning John Nash (1752-1835) to lay out Regent Street and Regent's Park in London, to design the celebrated "Pavilion" at Brighton and to turn Buckingham House into a Royal Palace. Admirable neither as a monarch nor as a man, George IV was at least an inspired patron and the most cultured King of England since Charles I.

The "most fantastic palace in Europe" — Brighton Pavilion.

GEORGE V
(1865–1936)

George V established the pattern for Britain's twentieth-century monarchy. His youth was passed in the navy (1877-92), but his preferred life-style was that of a Norfolk squire. Possessing a strong sense of public duty, George V was also greatly interested in the Empire, visiting India for the Delhi Durbar of 1911, the only "King/Emperor" to do so. In his tastes and outlook, the King was a traditionalist, but he readily accepted Britain's first

George V as Duke of York, 1893.

George V shaking hands with Bolton Wanderers at Wembley, 1926.

Labour Government. In times of political tension, such as the constitutional crisis of 1910-11 and the General Strike of 1926, his influence was exercised on behalf of moderation and compromise. His personal influence was also decisive in choosing Baldwin, rather than the aristocratic Curzon, as Prime Minister in 1923 and in persuading Ramsay MacDonald to form a National Government in 1931.

George V made the monarchy genuinely popular by participating in events that mattered to his subjects – visiting the trenches during the Great War or attending the first Wembley Cup Final in 1923. He also began the series of Christmas broadcasts which has continued ever since. The extent of his popularity was revealed by the celebrations of his jubilee year (1935). The King himself was genuinely surprised by the depth of the public's affection for him – "I can't understand it. I'm really quite an ordinary sort of chap." Perhaps that was the secret of his success.

GLADSTONE,
William Ewart
(1809-98)

Gladstone's name is almost inevitably linked with that of his arch rival, Disraeli, but the only qualities the two men had in common were immense political will-power, great skill in parliamentary debate and an intense mutual dislike. Disraeli could never match Gladstone's endless appetite for work nor his obsessive concern with administrative detail; nor did he share his crusading commitment to make Christian principles his basic guide in the conduct of public affairs.

The son of a wealthy Liverpool merchant, Gladstone was educated at Eton and Oxford, and, renouncing his early intention to enter the Church, became a Tory MP at the age of 23. A fervent admirer of Peel, he first made his reputation as Chancellor of the Exchequer under Aberdeen (1852-55), using his budgets to complete the movement towards Free Trade. Moving away from the Tories, like other Peelites, he was attracted by Palmerston's pro-Italian policy and joined his Cabinet in 1859, once again in the office of Chancellor. On Palmerston's death (1865), Gladstone emerged as leader of the new Liberal Party, a coalition of former Whigs and Peelites which drew its electoral support from Nonconformists, the Celtic areas and the business classes.

Dedicated to "Peace, Retrenchment and Reform", Gladstone's first ministry (1868-74) enacted a wide-ranging programme of

The Midlothian Campaign, 6 December 1879.

Gladstone in middle age.

split the party. Gladstone served a fourth term as Prime Minister (1892-94), again failing to carry "Home Rule" for Ireland, before retiring from office on grounds of age. At the time of his death the "G.O.M." (Grand Old Man), as journalists delighted to call him, was revered as a champion of individual conscience and of the rights of oppressed peoples. His literary output alone would have been a lifetime's work for most men; in fact, his career was marked by more practical reforms than that of any other politician of his times.

"He was generally thought to be very pusillanimous in dealing with foreign affairs. That is not at all the impression I derived. He was wholly ignorant." (Lord Cromer)

". . . that unprincipled maniac Gladstone — extraordinary mixture of envy, vindictiveness, hypocrisy and super- stition; and with one commanding characteristic — never a gentleman!" (Benjamin Disraeli)

". . . so very arrogant, tyrannical and obstinate with no knowledge of the World or human nature . . . a very dangerous and unsatisfactory Premier." (Queen Victoria)

institutional changes, affecting education, the legal system, the army, the civil service and the trade unions. It also introduced the secret ballot and tried to bring peace to Ireland by land reform and by ending state support for the Anglican church in that country. In 1875 Gladstone resigned the leadership of his party, but, outraged by the Bulgarian massacres (1876), emerged from retirement to lead a nation-wide agitation against Disraeli's foreign policy. His spectacular Midlothian campaign (1879) brought him back to power (1880-85) and a further bout of parliamentary reform. Against his personal inclination he felt obliged to intervene forcibly in Egyptian affairs. The death of General Gordon at Khartoum (1885), an indirect result of this intervention, brought him lasting unpopularity. In 1886 Gladstone's attempt to grant "Home Rule" to Ireland by giving it a separate parliament,

GORDON,
General Charles George ("Chinese Gordon," "Gordon of Khartoum") (1833-85)

Gordon was a regular army officer and that was almost the only thing that was regular about him. Having served as a Junior Officer in the Crimean War, he won lasting fame in the service of the Chinese Government by turning a rabble of mercenaries into an efficient and disciplined fighting unit, which crushed the Taiping rebels against which it was engaged. When his tour of duty was ended, Gordon characteristically refused the large sums offered to him (though he could not resist the yellow jacket of a high-ranking mandarin or the medal struck in his honour) and took up the obscure post of Commander of Engineers at Gravesend. His professional

duties leaving him much leisure, Gordon gave his spare time and most of his income to caring for and educating orphan boys. In 1873 Gordon entered the service of the Khedive Ismail of Egypt and devoted the next seven years of his life to suppressing the slave-trade and imposing the authority of his employer across the million square miles of the Sudan. His departure was followed by a popular rising, led by the Mahdi, a religious leader who believed he had a mission to establish God's kingdom on earth. With the consent of the British Government, Gordon accepted the task of organizing the withdrawal of the Egyptian administration from the Sudan. A partial evacuation was carried out, but Gordon himself, against orders and with a reduced garrison, attempted to hold

The death of Gordon at Khartoum.

A sketch by Edward Clifford.

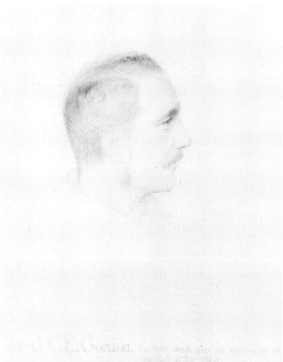

the capital, Khartoum, against the Mahdi's forces. After a siege of 317 days the city fell and Gordon found the martyr's death he had perhaps been seeking. A fervent Christian, utterly indifferent to danger and death, Gordon had an iron sense of duty — but always decided himself where that duty lay. To his political masters he was a vexatious puzzle, to the Victorian public a shining hero.

From Gordon's diary, September — November 1884:

"I am not the *rescued lamb*, and I will not be."

"It is quite painful to see men tremble so when they come to see me, that they cannot hold the match to their cigarette."

"Better a ball in the brain than to flicker out unheeded."

GRACE,
W. G.
(1848-1915)

W. G. Grace transformed cricket from a village pastime into a national institution. A surgeon by profession, he made his first appearance in a "Gentlemen versus Players" match at the age of 17 and played his last first-class match at the age of 60. In the course of his career he scored 54,896 runs, including 126 centuries, and took 2,876 wickets. A considerable bowler and a cunning

W. G. Grace, painted by an unknown artist.

captain, Grace was supreme as a batsman. In the first Test Match to be played in England against Australia he made 152. At the height of his powers, in 1876, he made 400 not out and then, in three successive innings, scored 344, 177 and 318 not out.

A giant of a man, with a great, flowing black beard, "W. G." caught the imagination of late Victorian England. Thanks largely to his exploits, the game of cricket began to attract regular press coverage and financial support. Grace himself founded the Gloucestershire county eleven in 1870 and visited Australia in 1873 and again in 1891. In 1895 the *Daily Telegraph* organized a fund in his honour which raised £5,000. Neville Cardus, the greatest of all cricket writers, summarized the importance of Grace's career as follows:

W. G. came forward at a ripe moment; the technique of cricket stood ready for expansion and masterly summary; the period was also ready for a game which everybody could watch, the gentry as well as the increasing population of town workers. Grace's skill as a batsman may be said to have orchestrated the simple folk-song of the game; his personality placed it on the country's stage.

Victorian cricket — a match at Torquay.

HARDIE,
James Keir
(1856–1915)

Britain's first socialist Member of Parliament began work in a Scottish coal-mine at the age of 10. He learned the art of public speaking through the temperance movement, became a trade unionist and in 1888 established the Scottish Parliamentary Labour Party, standing

Keir Hardie addressing a Suffragettes' Free Speech meeting in Trafalgar Square, May 1913.

NOT A WISE SAW

Mr. Keir Hardie wishes to make Labour representation entirely independent of the Liberal Party.

Cartoon of 1903.

for mid-Lanark in a by-election as the first Labour candidate ever in any British constituency. From 1892 to 1895 he served as Independent Socialist MP for West Ham South. In 1893 he founded the Independent Labour Party and in 1900 played a leading part in setting up the Labour Representation Committee, the immediate ancestor of today's Labour Party. As Member of Parliament for Merthyr Tydfil (1900-15), Keir Hardie became Chairman of the Parliamentary Labour Party in 1906 and vigorously asserted its independence from the Liberals, whose government it generally supported. At the same time he worked to strengthen the ties between the party and the trade union movement. A convinced pacifist, he was also a supporter of women's rights.

HILL,
Sir Rowland
(1795-1879)

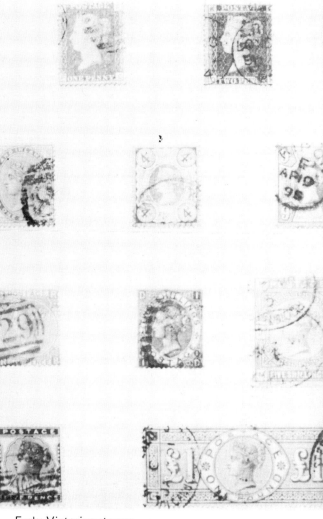

A man of wide interests, ranging from railways and printing to astronomy, education and the colonization of Australia, Sir Rowland Hill is chiefly remembered as the originator of the modern postal system. His ideas, put forward in a pamphlet, *Post Office Reform* (1837), were basically simple — postal charges should be low (to encourage a high volume of mail, and therefore greater revenue), uniform,

Sir Rowland Hill.

Early Victorian stamps.

regardless of distance (to save on expensive accounting), and pre-paid (to avoid loss and simplify administration). Payment was to be signified by means of Hill's ingenious invention — the postage stamp. Despite opposition, Hill's ideas were put into effect in 1840 and soon proved to be of immense social and economic benefit to the nation. Hill was knighted in 1860, in recognition of the importance of his work, and his system was adopted world-wide in the course of the following century.

HITCHCOCK,
Sir Alfred
(1899–1980)

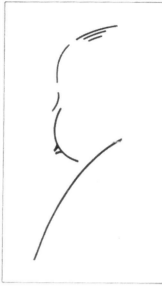

Britain's most distinguished film director began his career by painting the backgrounds for silent film titles. After working in a German studio, Hitchcock made his first important film, *The Lodger*, in 1927. Like most of his later works, it was a suspense story about an ordinary person caught up in extraordinary events. He then made *Blackmail*, the first British feature film with sound. His success with such thrillers as *The Thirty Nine*

A 1959 photograph of Alfred Hitchcock and the line drawing which was used as the logo for his television series in America.

Filming *The Birds*.

Steps (1935) and *The Lady Vanishes* (1938) led to his being invited to work in Hollywood, where most of the rest of his sixty films were made. Two only can be mentioned as classic examples of Hitchcock's style — *North by North West* (1959), with its fantastic chase sequences, and *Psycho* (1960), for its intense study of the psychology of fear and guilt. "Hitch" was a unique figure in the history of film, for he was both a superb entertainer, content to reach a mass audience through the commercial cinema, and also a director whose work was widely praised by critics and film-makers, not only in English-speaking countries but in France as well.

HOGARTH,
William
(1697-1764)

Apprenticed to a silversmith, from whom he learned the art of engraving, Hogarth first established himself as a book-illustrator and

From *The Rake's Progress.*

then, after studying painting, as a portrait painter. Unwilling to flatter his subjects, he made little progress but turned instead to the everyday world around him. Unlike most artists of his day, Hogarth found subjects for pictures not in history or classical mythology but in the streets of London. Many of his paintings satirize the vanity and greed of fashionable society and some of the most famous tell a story, scene by scene. *The Rake's Progress* (1733) shows the decline of a foolish young man who squanders his inheritance and ends in a

Hogarth at work, an engraving after a self portrait of about 1757.

lunatic asylum. *Marriage à la Mode* (1745) chronicles the quarrels which follow from a match for money, not love. These "modern moral subjects", as Hogarth called them, proved extremely popular with the newly affluent middle class, who recognized in them a view of life which they could appreciate and understand. Perhaps they were also attracted by Hogarth's common-sense disapproval of snobbish airs and his dislike of foreign fashions. Because Hogarth's pictures were widely and cheaply available in the form of engravings, his work has become much better known than that of artists who worked only in oils. And, as the writer Charles Lamb said of him: "other pictures we look at — his prints we read".

HOWARD,
Sir Ebenezer
(1850–1928)

A London-born shorthand-reporter, Howard emigrated to America (1872-79), where he was deeply influenced by the poetry of Emerson, Lowell and Whitman, all of whom stressed the importance of man's relation to nature. Howard was also impressed by Edward Bellamy's *Looking Backward* (1888), a work which also inspired William Morris, with its vision of a future in which man and nature lived in harmony. Howard

Ebenezer Howard.

Welwyn Garden City.

saw around him an England in which the countryside was drained of its youngest and healthiest by migration and in which the overcrowded cities forced upon men an environment in which it was impossible to live a fulfilled and healthy life. Howard's remedy was the "garden city", a planned community in which industrial and residential needs would be harmonized and easy access to natural surroundings maintained. These ideas were set out in *Tomorrow*, published in 1898 and republished in 1902 as *Garden Cities of Tomorrow*. In 1899 Howard formed the Garden City Association to give practical expression to his theories. Letchworth and Welwyn Garden City, both in Hertfordshire, are the most clear evidence of Howard's work, but his influence on town-planning has been of international importance in the twentieth century.

JENNER,
Edward
(1749–1823)

The discoverer of vaccination was, and remained all his life, a simple country doctor. Trained in London by the famous surgeon, John Hunter (1728-93), Jenner returned to practise in his native village of Berkeley, Gloucestershire. Here, careful observation over many years led him to conclude that the reason why milkmaids were rarely afflicted by the scourge of smallpox was that they contracted the milder "cowpox" from their

A bronze statue of Jenner vaccinating a child.

animals and this gave them some form of protection. In 1796 Jenner tested his theory by deliberately inserting cowpox matter into scratches made on the arm of a healthy boy of 8. Some months later the boy was inoculated with smallpox and proved entirely resistant to it. Jenner's discovery was published in 1798 and, despite the opposition of the medical profession, the practice of vaccination spread rapidly. It is estimated that by 1800 100,000 people had been vaccinated. In 1807 Bavaria became the first state to make vaccination compulsory. In England it was generally enforced from 1872 onwards. Acclaimed by a grateful public, awarded honorary degrees by the universities of Oxford and Harvard, and granted £30,000 by Parliament in recognition of his discovery, Jenner remained quietly in his country practice until his death.

JOHNSON,
Dr Samuel
(1709–84)

Having failed as a schoolmaster and as a playwright, Dr Johnson won enduring fame as the compiler of the first true dictionary of the English language. Poverty prevented him from completing his studies at Oxford and throughout the eight years during which he was working on his dictionary he was obliged to

Johnson with Boswell, a cartoon by Rowlandson.

A "district vaccinator" at work in London's East End, 1871.

Johnson's statue in his home town of Lichfield.

support himself by writing essays on political and literary topics. In 1763 Johnson met James Boswell, a young Scot who dutifully recorded the details of Johnson's conversations, opinions and friendships. Boswell's *Life of Johnson* (1791) makes him one of the best-known and most often quoted figures in English literature. A staunch Tory in politics, Johnson loved food, drink and good company but worked prodigiously as well, producing a complete edition of Shakespeare's works, a series of *Lives of the Poets* and a novel, *Rasselas*, written in a month to pay the expenses of his mother's funeral. A master of English prose, Johnson read widely, remembered well and had a genius for making clear definitions and distinctions. His great *Dictionary* stood for more than a century not merely as a work of reference but also as a work of art.

> "There is no arguing with Johnson; for if his pistol misses fire, he knocks you down with the butt end of it." (Oliver Goldsmith)
>
> ---
>
> "The reputation of those writings, which he probably expected to be immortal, is every day fading; while those peculiarities of manner and that careless table-talk the memory of which, he probably thought, would die with him, are likely to be remembered as long as the English language is spoken in any quarter of the globe." (T. B. Macaulay)

VERY.

ed that I should have been guilty of such a riot
rose I went into D' Johnsons room
ntieth Sunday after Trinity in the epistle for which

KEYNES,
J. M.
(1883-1946)

John Maynard Keynes did more to change economics than any other single man since Adam Smith. Educated at Eton and Cambridge, he spent the early years of his career at the India Office and as a university lecturer.

After serving on the Royal Commission on Indian Finance and Currency, he entered the Treasury in 1915 and served as its main representative at the Paris Peace Conference in 1919. He disagreed strongly with the harsh attitudes of the Allies on such issues as frontier revision and reparations payments and resigned his position to write *The Economic Consequences of the Peace*, a brilliant denunciation of the leading statesmen and their policies.

During the 1920s Keynes associated himself with the Liberal Party and advocated an unorthodox policy of curing the general economic depression by a massive programme of public investment to be paid for out of

Unemployed, 1930s.

J. M. Keynes.

KIPLING,
Rudyard
(1865–1936)

Born in Bombay, but educated in England, Joseph Rudyard Kipling joined the staff of the *Lahore Civil and Military Gazette* at the age of 17 and gradually established a reputation for himself as a writer of verse and short stories. He reached the height of his popularity in the 1890s with the publication of his *Barrack Room Ballads*, the two *Jungle Books* and *Captains Courageous*. The main themes of his work were family and Empire.

Rudyard Kipling, portrait by Sir Philip Burne-Jones, 1899.

taxes and government borrowing. This revision of conventional economic wisdom was presented at length in Keynes' most famous work, *The General Theory of Employment, Interest and Money* (1936). Keynes' basic argument was that no economy had any natural or automatic tendency towards full employment, but that this could be achieved by government intervention. At first, this view was regarded as controversial, but it rapidly became the general basis of post-war economic policies among the industrial democracies. During the Second World War Keynes returned to the Treasury as the government's chief adviser on financial matters. Created Baron Keynes in 1942, he played a leading part in the Bretton Woods Conference (1944) which led to the creation of the International Monetary Fund. Keynes' personal interests were artistic and cultural. Having made a large fortune through investments and foreign currency dealings, he became a collector of rare books and paintings. The philosopher Bertrand Russell said of Keynes that his "intellect was the sharpest and clearest that I have ever known".

His heroes stood for duty, justice and loyalty, representing virtues that appealed to many readers. Kipling's strong sense of poetic rhythm and his vivid descriptive prose also made him a writer whom the ordinary reader felt he could understand. Too often regarded as a simple-minded imperialist, Kipling was acutely aware of both the corruptions and responsibilities of power — as ''Recessional'', the poem he wrote for Queen Victoria's Diamond Jubilee, so clearly shows. He considered it his finest work, but he is probably best remembered for his much-quoted ''If''.

Kipling was fascinated by India, its vastness and its variety. Like many of his countrymen, he saw the English as new Romans, imposing order firmly but fairly, to establish peace and justice in savage regions. But, despite the fact that he left India for good at the age of 24, he retained a real capacity to see Indian life through Indian eyes, and a number of critics have praised *Kim* (1901), his novel of suspense and adventure, as the best fictional work on India written in English. Refusing both the laureateship and the Order of Merit, Kipling was awarded the Nobel Prize for Literature in 1907, although by then his popularity had already begun to wane.

''On the brain'' by Phil May.

From ''Tiger — Tiger'', chapter 2 of the first *Jungle Book*, illustrated by W. H. Drake.

KITCHENER,
Field Marshal Earl
(1850–1916)

A career soldier, Irish-born Kitchener served as an engineer and surveyor in Palestine, Cyprus and the Sudan before taking command of the army in Egypt. His victory over the Mahdi's dervish army at Omdurman (1898) and his re-conquest of the Sudan made him a national hero. As Commander-in-Chief during the Boer War in South Africa (1899-1902) he was criticized for his policy of herding civilians into "concentration camps" to deprive the Boer guerillas of support and supplies. As head of the Indian army, Kitchener quarrelled, successfully, with the Viceroy, Lord Curzon,

Kitchener of Khartoum.

A recruiting poster for Kitchener's "New Army".

about the limits of his power. From 1911 to 1914 he served as British Agent in Egypt, where his power had no limits. This was a poor preparation for his supreme command, as War Minister in Asquith's Cabinet, a position in which he had to learn to get along with his political colleagues. But Kitchener never did learn and seemed to make little effort to do so. His relations with the generals were not much better. However, he did realize that the "Great War" would not be "over by Christmas" and his public popularity enabled him to call for volunteers by the million. Most of them went into action in France in 1916, the year in which the creator of Britain's first mass army drowned when HMS *Hampshire*, taking him on a mission to Russia, struck a mine. Efficient, reserved and ruthless, Kitchener was liked by few who knew him and worshipped by millions who did not.

LANSBURY,
George
(1859-1940)

As a Christian and a socialist, George Lansbury was a champion both of the poor and of causes, such as pacifism and women's suffrage, which they generally despised. Born in Suffolk, Lansbury became active in the local politics of London's East End. As a member of the Royal Commission on the Poor Law (1905-9), he signed the famous "Minority Report" which called for more generous

George Lansbury.

treatment of the destitute. As Mayor of Poplar (1921), he was to defy government policy by leading a protest against the unequal rate burden on London's rich and poor boroughs. Thirty councillors were imprisoned, but the rate burden was adjusted and Poplar and other councils continued to pay their poor and unemployed more than was officially approved by the central government.

Despite having had only an elementary school education, Lansbury became founder and first editor of the *Daily Herald* (1919-23), Britain's first left-wing national daily newspaper. Having served in MacDonald's second government (1920-31), Lansbury was the only Labour minister not to lose his seat in the election of 1931. After serving as Leader of the Labour Party and Opposition from 1931-35, he was ousted by trade unionists, such as Bevin, who were looking for a less gentle man. A non-smoker and tee-totaller, Lansbury stood for an emotional and homely sort of socialism which made him loved rather than respected.

LAWRENCE,
T. E. ("Lawrence of Arabia")
(1888-1935)

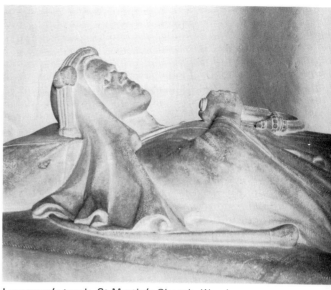

Thomas Edward Lawrence was a man who became first a legend and then its victim. An early interest in archaeology led him to the Middle East, where he became a fluent speaker of Arabic and, on the outbreak of war, an intelligence officer in Cairo. In December 1916 he was sent to Jedda, where the Emir Feisal (later King of Iraq) and his father, Hussein, had risen against the rule of the

Lawrence's tomb, St Martin's Church, Wareham.

Arab cavalry await battle.

Ottoman Turks. Lawrence played a leading part in the Arabs' guerilla campaign, raiding the Damascus-Medina railway and seizing a number of strategic centres, such as the Red Sea port of Aqaba. These hit-and-run tactics, by drawing off Turkish troops from the main theatre of war, aided the advance of the British General Allenby's army from Egypt into Palestine.

In a military sense, the "Arab revolt" was a side-show. The British public, however, eager for victories in the disastrous year 1917, thrilled to newspaper reports of the daring raids of an Oxford scholar turned Bedouin. Lawrence found himself cast in the role of mysterious hero and enjoyed it — at first.

Lawrence also encouraged the Arabs' political ambitions, which focused on the creation of a large independent Arab state. When the peace treaties gave Syria to France and Palestine to Britain, as League of Nations' mandates, Lawrence considered that the Arab cause had been betrayed, although he did assist Churchill (Colonial Secretary, 1921-22) in reconciling the Arabs to the terms of the settlement. He then retired from public life, refusing all honours, and enlisted under assumed names, first in the Tank Corps and then in the RAF, until he was killed in a motor cycle accident. His account of the Arab revolt, *The Seven Pillars of Wisdom*, was printed privately in 1926, but not published until after his death. The extravagant tone of the dedication of his book reveals Lawrence's love of drama and romance: "I drew these tides of men into my hands and wrote my will across the sky in stars". He was a proud, brilliant and unhappy man. Lord Vansittart, the diplomat, said of him that he "was one of the people I was glad to have known and not to have known better". Lawrence might have been pleased to say the same about himself.

LEVER,
W. H. (Viscount Leverhulme of the Western Isles) (1851-1925)

Born the son of a Bolton grocer, William Hesketh Lever entered his father's business at the age of 16 and was made a full partner five years later. In 1884 Lever and his brother went into business on their own account, specializing in a soap called "Sunlight". In 1888 the firm founded a new town, Port Sunlight, in Cheshire to house their works and workers. This became a model settlement to which Lever made many gifts, including public gardens and an art gallery. In 1894 the firm of Lever Bros. became a public company which, in the course of time, became the giant Unilever corporation, now one of Britain's largest businesses. Lever, who sat as a Liberal MP from 1906 to 1909, also established the Leverhulme Trust, which has given millions of pounds to promote research and education.

Park Road, Port Sunlight.

Viscount Leverhulme, 1919.

LIVINGSTONE,
David
(1813-73)

This most famous of Victorian missionaries was born at Blantyre, Lanarkshire, and went to work in a cotton mill at the age of ten. By his own efforts, he acquired an education and, in 1840, having qualified as a medical missionary, he was sent to Bechuanaland. Becoming convinced of his destiny to explore the interior of Africa, at that time unknown to Europeans, he set out on a major expedition in 1853, intending to find a practical route between the west coast and his own area of missionary activity around the headwaters

Rev. David Livingstone.

of the Zambezi. In the course of his three-year wanderings he crossed Africa from the Atlantic to the Indian Ocean, tracing the course of the Zambezi from its source to its mouth, and becoming the first European to see the Victoria Falls.

Livingstone's account of this journey, *Missionary Travels and Researches in South Africa* (1857), became a best-seller and made him enough money to retire on. But in 1858 he accepted a commission from the British Government to explore eastern and central Africa. His sighting of Lake Nyasa in the course of his second expedition proved to be less important to him than his experience of the impact of Arab slave-raids. As a result of what he saw, Livingstone became obsessed with the need to wipe out the slave trade for good, and this became a major objective of his third expedition, which left Zanzibar in 1866. His other great aim was to find the source of the Nile and in this he failed.

Livingstone's party soon lost all contact with the outside world and suffered dreadful hardships. An American newspaper at last organized a relief expedition, led by the journalist, H. M. Stanley, who finally found Livingstone in 1871. Broken in health, the explorer died in 1873. His African servants carried his embalmed body a thousand miles to the coast for eventual interment in Westminster Abbey. But his heart was buried in Africa.

> "I never met a man who fulfilled more completely my idea of a perfect Christian gentleman." (Sir Bartle Frere, *Proceedings of the Royal Geographical Society*, 1874)

Victoria Falls, Zambesi, from Livingstone's *Missionary Travels and Researches in South Africa*, published in 1857.

LLOYD GEORGE, David (1863-1945)

This most famous of Welsh politicians was in fact born in Manchester. Brought up in relative poverty in North Wales, he had only a village schooling, but qualified as a solicitor before being elected MP for Caernarvon in 1890. He soon showed himself to be a brilliant speaker, whether in English or Welsh, in the House of

Lloyd George, 1924, at Chequers.

THE PHILANTHROPIC HIGHWAYMAN.

Mr. Lloyd George. "I'll make 'em pity the aged poor!"

Punch's view of old age pensions, 5 August 1908.

Commons or on an open hill-side. He became notorious for his outspoken criticism of the Boer War, but was nevertheless appointed President of the Board of Trade and later Chancellor of the Exchequer (1908-15). In 1904 he had warned that "you cannot feed the hungry on statistics" and, as Chancellor, he pioneered such major social reforms as old age pensions (1908) and national health insurance (1911). His "People's Budget" (1909), which proposed a super-tax on high incomes and land-value duties to finance spending on social welfare, led to a constitutional crisis which was resolved by the Parliament Act of 1911. Unwise dealings in the shares of the Marconi wireless company led to charges of corruption being brought against him in 1914 but, with the help of the Prime Minister, Asquith, his name was cleared.

Following the "shell scandal", which revealed the inefficiency of war-time production methods, Lloyd George was appointed as the first ever Minister of Munitions in 1915. He then intrigued with the Conservatives to overthrow and replace Asquith as Prime

Minister (1916). Lloyd George undoubtedly made the conduct of the war more vigorous and effective, but his unscrupulous treatment of Asquith was never forgiven by many Liberals.

As war leader, Lloyd George successfully pressed the navy to take up the convoy system, but had great difficulty in influencing the strategy of his generals, although he did eventually persuade them to accept the overall command of Marshal Foch on the Western Front. Lloyd George's diplomatic skills were employed to advantage both at the Paris Peace Conference (1919), where he modified some of the harsher proposals of the Treaty of Versailles, and in negotiating the partition of Ireland (1921) into Ulster and an independent Irish Free State. Allegations of corruption were revived against Lloyd George at this time, as a result of his distribution of honours and titles in return for contributions to party funds. The fact that these went mostly to the Liberals naturally vexed the Conservatives, who took the opportunity of the Chanak crisis (1922), which brought Britain to the brink of war against Turkey, to withdraw from the coalition and force Lloyd George from office. The "Welsh Wizard" never held power again; and nor did the Liberal Party.

> "Lloyd George is rooted in nothing, he is void and without content . . . he is an instrument and a player at the same time which plays on the company and is played on by them too . . . a vampire and a medium in one." (J. M. Keynes)
>
> ---
>
> "A master of improvised speech and improvised policies." (A. J. P. Taylor, *English History 1914-1945*)

MACAULAY,
Thomas Babington
(1800-59)

T. B. Macaulay was a precociously clever schoolboy who became a precociously clever man. He learned to read at the age of three and entered Parliament at the age of thirty, having already established a literary reputation as an essayist and reviewer in the pages of the *Edinburgh Review*. Pitched into the struggle over the great Reform Bill, he spoke brilliantly on behalf of the "Magna Carta of the middle class", although he himself stood for one of the rottenest of rotten boroughs.

From 1834 to 1838 Macaulay worked as a member of the Supreme Council of India, drafting a new penal code almost single-

Macaulay, portrait by John Partridge, c.1849-53.

handed and in sublime and wilful ignorance of the customs and culture of the people for whom it was intended. (Lord Melbourne is supposed to have remarked on one occasion that "I wish I were as sure of one thing as Tom Macaulay is of everything".) Macaulay also drew up an extremely influential Minute on educational policy, which dismissed all Hindu, Buddhist and Islamic learning as worthless and confidently recommended the complete adoption of European curricula and teaching methods.

In Parliament, Macaulay was an effective and respected speaker and a strong supporter of factory reform and measures to enlarge the civil rights of Catholics and Jews. After serving for a year in Lord John Russell's Cabinet (1846-47), Macaulay turned from politics to devote himself to his monumental *History of England* (1849-55). Written in magnificent prose, after immensely thorough research, it was intended to cover the history of the nation since 1685, but in fact never got beyond 1697. It was nevertheless hailed as a masterpiece and exerted a lasting influence on the way Englishmen saw their history and therefore England as a nation. Macaulay had once remarked in reviewing a book by another author that "the history of England is emphatically the history of progress" and his own *History* was an emphatic attempt to support that viewpoint. The book provided his middle-class readers with a triumphant account of their rise to power, and also contributed to the growth of imperialist sentiment, because its assertion of English superiority implied a special sense of mission and the right of Englishmen to order the lives of others, as Macaulay himself had done in India.

Lord Macaulay's library.

MacDONALD,
James Ramsay
(1866-1937)

Impoverished and illegitimate by birth, Ramsay MacDonald rose from the obscurity of a Scottish fishing village to head Britain's first Labour Government and then to split the party for a decade. From 1900 to 1912 he acted as Honorary Secretary of the infant Labour Party, being elected to Parliament in 1906. Leader of the Labour Party in the Commons from 1911 to 1914, he lost influence on account of his pacifist views during the Great War and was out of Parliament from 1918 to 1922, when he became Leader of the Opposition. In 1924 he headed the short-lived Labour minority government and in 1929 returned to power as Britain plunged into the worst phase of the interwar depression. The financial crisis of 1931 led him to form a coalition National Government which most Labour MPs refused to support. As Prime Minister until 1935, MacDonald exercised considerable influence in foreign affairs but continued to be regarded as a traitor to the party by most of his former colleagues. Silver-haired and silver-tongued, Ramsay MacDonald was overwhelmed by the fact of his own success. He was, as Beatrice Webb put it, "a magnificent substitute for a leader".

James Ramsay MacDonald, portrait by Sir John Lavery, 1931.

Ramsay MacDonald, 26 June 1933, at the Lord Mayor's banquet for delegates of the World Economic Conference.

MALTHUS,
Rev. T. R.
(1776-1834)

Malthus' *Essay on the Principle of Population as it affects the future Improvement of Society* (1798) has been one of the most influential works of modern times. It was written to challenge the optimistic belief that an ideal form of society can be produced merely by encouraging men to follow their natural desires. Malthus argued that, far from this being the case, life was inevitably "a perpetual struggle for room and food" and there was an unavoidable tendency for food supplies to expand less rapidly than population. In the long run, in Malthus' view, human populations would always be in balance with the food supplies necessary to maintain them,

Rev. T. R. Malthus.

because the surplus of people would be eliminated by such "positive checks" as war, famine and epidemic disease. The operation of these positive checks might, however, be modified by "preventive checks" such as late marriage and small families. Any policies which discouraged the operation of these "preventive checks", such as a poor relief system which enabled labourers to have families larger than they could support, would only aggravate rather than relieve the problem of poverty. Malthus' *Essay* was widely read and his ideas, which were used to justify the harsh "New Poor Law" of 1834, helped to gain economics the title of "the dismal science". Malthus failed to foresee the immense improvements which took place in agriculture in the nineteenth century, but the "population explosion" of our own times has given his views a new currency.

The nightmare come true — Irish peasants outside a workhouse, 1846.

MARLBOROUGH,
John Churchill, First Duke of
(1650–1722)

Blenheim Palace.

The most renowned soldier of his day, John Churchill also showed himself to be a skilled diplomat and a forceful, if not entirely successful, politician. Having served with distinction under the great French commander, Turenne, and married the talented Sarah Jennings, lady-in-waiting to the future Queen Anne, he rose through the favour of

Marlborough in triumph, painted by Sir Godfrey Kneller, c. 1706.

the Duke of York, the later James II, to become a peer and a general at the age of 32. Despite his support for William III during the revolution of 1688, Marlborough fell from favour until the formation of the Grand Alliance (Britain, Austria and the Netherlands) brought him once more to prominence. In the War of Spanish Succession (1702-13) Marlborough led the Anglo-Dutch forces in ten victorious campaigns against the armies of Louis XIV, winning memorable victories at Blenheim (1704), Ramillies (1706), Oudenarde (1708) and Malplaquet (1709) and conducting eighteen successful sieges. Political intrigues at the English court led to his dismissal in 1711, but Blenheim Palace in Oxfordshire stands as a testimony to a grateful nation's lasting admiration for his cold courage and great abilities.

MAUDSLAY,
Henry
(1771-1831)

This great mechanical engineer was born at the Woolwich Arsenal, where he acquired such fame as a metal-worker that the inventor Joseph Bramah (1748-1814) sent for him and eventually made him his head foreman. Once in business on his own account, Maudslay produced a number of significant inventions of his own. His first was the slide-rest, which enabled metal-workers using a lathe to clamp the cutting tool against the revolving metal they wished to shape and thus to produce a more accurate result with far less physical effort. Next came an all-metal lathe, for

Maudslay's lathe with slide rest (marked "h").

Henry Maudslay, 1827.

cutting screws, and a bench micrometer, for measuring to a high degree of precision. Maudslay's most important single project was to build the 43 machines designed by Sir Marc Brunel (1769-1849) to mechanize the manufacture of pulley-blocks for warships. The work took six years, and the machines, installed at Portsmouth dockyard, were the world's first successful example of integrated mass-production. In 1810 Maudslay went into partnership with Joshua Field (1787-1863), to specialize in making marine engines. Maudslay also invented a machine for printing textiles and another for softening water by aeration. His workshops trained some of the most illustrious engineers of the Victorian period, including Isambard Kingdom Brunel (1803-87), Joseph Whitworth (1803-87), who introduced the standardized screw head thread, and James Nasmyth (1808-90), who invented the steam hammer.

MILL,
John Stuart
(1806-73)

Rigorously educated by his father, who was an earnest disciple of Jeremy Bentham, John Stuart Mill had, by his own reckoning, at 20, a quarter of a century's head-start over young men of his own age. After passing through an immense mental crisis of depression, Mill came, under the influence of his friend, Harriet Taylor, to develop a more humane form of Bentham's utilitarian philosophy.

Punch cartoon, 1867.

Mill emphasized, above all, the value of human freedom and the worth and significance of the individual. As he put it in his famous essay, *On Liberty* (1859), "the worth of a State, in the long run, is the worth of the individuals composing it". Fearful of the tyranny of majority opinion in an age of growing democracy, Mill warned that the dissenting opinions of minorities must be cherished — "We can never be sure that the opinion we are endeavouring to stifle is a false opinion; and if we were sure, stifling it would be an evil still." Mill is now regarded as one of the giants of the liberal tradition and his ideas about the value of free speech have become generally accepted in modern democracies. His writings on logic, economics and philosophy won him enormous respect among his contemporaries, but towards the end of his life, when he began to favour

MILL'S LOGIC; OR, FRANCHISE FOR FEMALES.
"PRAY CLEAR THE WAY, THERE, FOR THESE—A—PERSONS."

socialism and to support women's rights, he was looked upon with increasing suspicion and even ridicule. A man of affairs, as well as of ideas, Mill was for long a leading official of the East India Company (1823-58) and, briefly (1865-68), Radical MP for Westminster. Brought up without religious belief, Mill impressed even the pious Gladstone as "the Saint of Rationalism".

MONTGOMERY,
Bernard Law (Field Marshal Montgomery of Alamein) (1887-1976)

"Monty" was Britain's most successful twentieth-century general. He was not merely a professional soldier, but *the* professional soldier, dedicated to his vocation. He served on the Western Front throughout most of the Great War and was promoted steadily to become Commander of the Third Division of the British Expeditionary Force at the beginning of the Second World War. Montgomery made his reputation with the Eighth Army in North Africa, Sicily and Italy. He then commanded Allied troops during the Normandy landings (1944) and played the decisive part in turning back the German counter-attack in the Ardennes. In May 1945 he formally accepted the surrender of all German forces in NW Europe at Lüneburg Heath. From 1951 to 1958 he served as Deputy Supreme Commander of NATO.

John Stuart Mill, painted by George Frederic Watts, 1873.

Montgomery of Alamein, portrait by Frank O. Salisbury, 1945.

Montgomery's special qualities were immense thoroughness in preparing for set-piece battles, such as El Alamein (1942), and an ability to convey to the men under his command an understanding of the part they were to play in the great conflict in which they were engaged. A non-smoker and tee-totaller, Montgomery set his men an outstanding example of physical fitness and mental alertness. But, as Field Marshal Alexander once noted, "he was not an easy man to deal with".

Allied Commander Montgomery, with liaison officers.

MORRIS,
William
(1834–96)

Poet, designer, craftsman and socialist, William Morris was as restless as he was versatile, as unconventional as he was kind-hearted. Expelled from Marlborough for his part in a school rebellion, Morris was indifferent to his studies at Oxford, but made himself an expert on English medieval crafts and architecture and revealed an early talent for writing verse. Falling under the influence of the poet Dante Gabriel Rossetti (1828-82), Morris joined the group of young artists

The Socialist League, Hammersmith. Morris is fourth from the right in the second row.

Working drawings for wallpaper designs by William Morris, 1873-74 — ''Pimpernel'', ''Acanthus'' and ''African Marigold''.

William Morris, 1889.

known as the Pre-Raphaelite Brotherhood and began to study painting. In 1861 he established "The Firm", to produce craft goods and church ornaments of the highest artistic standard. In 1869 he published "The Earthly Paradise", a long allegorical poem which brought him fame and the offer of the Professorship of Poetry at Oxford, an offer he declined. Convinced that the greed and exploitation which he saw around him could only lead to the production of shoddy goods and corrupt works of art, Morris turned to socialism. A tireless member of the Social Democratic Federation and the Socialist League until his health failed, Morris lectured, organized and wrote extensively for the socialist cause. Best remembered as a writer for *News from Nowhere* (1891), a fantasy about Britain after the socialist revolution, Morris is also commemorated as an artist by his designs for textiles and wallpapers and by his efforts, at the Kelmscott Press, to revive the art of printing beautiful books. He was also an early pioneer of the conservation of ancient buildings. Morris, for all his love of the medieval period, was not a mere reactionary and opponent of technology. He believed that men should live in harmony with their creation, rather than being dominated by it. Morris's designs have long been appreciated; the modern relevance of his ideas is only beginning to be understood.

> "I can't understand how a man who . . . enjoys dinner — and breakfast — and supper — to that extent of fat — can write such lovely poems about Misery." (John Ruskin)
>
> ---
>
> "You can lose a man like that by your own death, but not by his." (George Bernard Shaw)
>
> ---
>
> "The one perfectly happy and fortunate poet of modern times."(W. B. Yeats)

MORRISON,
Herbert (Lord Morrison of Lambeth) (1888–1965)

The son of a London policeman with strong Tory views, Morrison came into Labour politics through local government and remained strongly linked with the London County Council throughout his life. A master of administration, with a great appetite for work, Morrison served as Minister of Transport

1940. Herbert Morrison walking to the Labour Party office.

in Ramsay MacDonald's second government, reorganizing London's transport system. As Home Secretary in Churchill's war-time government, he was virtual dictator on the home front. As the main architect of Labour's 1945 election victory, he was generally regarded as one of the three most powerful leaders of the Attlee government. In this period his major achievement was to guide Labour's massive programme of welfare and nationalization through Parliament. After serving briefly as Foreign Secretary in 1951, he was made a peer in 1959. A man of little education, with no claim to being a thinker, Morrison was popular within the party, but not with his colleagues. Bevin, in particular, maintained a long-standing feud with him. Yet there were many similarities between them, for both enjoyed the exercise of power.

MOUNTBATTEN,
Lord Louis (Earl Mountbatten of Burma) (1900-79)

A professional sailor, Mountbatten served in the North Sea during the First World War and, at the beginning of the Second, commanded a destroyer flotilla, his own ship, HMS *Kelly*, being sunk off Crete in 1941. As Chief of Combined Operations, Mountbatten helped to plan the raids on St Nazaire and Dieppe (1942) and to prepare for the D-Day invasion

Lord and Lady Mountbatten after they had been sworn in as Viceroy and Vicereine of India. He is wearing admiral's uniform

served as First Sea Lord (1955-59) and Chief of the Defence Staff (1959-65). In retirement he devoted special concern to the United World Colleges movement, dedicated to the education of young people from all countries in an international environment. Lord Louis Mountbatten was assassinated, along with other members of his family, when a bomb was placed aboard his sailing-boat by members of an Irish terrorist organization.

> "Mountbatten proved a heavy-weight figure. . . . He was a scientifically-minded commander. . . . He had a gift for the use of public relations. . . . He had in fact something of the personal glamour of a film star. . . ." (Peter Calvocoressi and Guy Wint, *Total War*)

Earl Mountbatten of Burma, Admiral of the Fleet, painted by John Ulbricht, 1968.

of 1944. Appointed Supreme Allied Commander, SE Asia in 1943, he directed the counter-attack which drove the Japanese from Burma, and accepted the surrender of all their forces in the region in September 1945. In February 1947 Mountbatten was appointed as the last Viceroy of India, with the task of overseeing the transition to independence. In a tense political situation, he impressed the leaders of all parties with his energy and sincerity and was invited to serve as the first Governor-General of independent India. Resuming his naval career, Mountbatten

NASH,
John
(1752-1835)

Born the son of a millwright, John Nash became one of the most successful architects of his day. His first venture as a speculative builder ended in bankruptcy, but he managed to establish a reputation as an architect by designing country houses in Wales and the West of England. Success came to Nash through his partnership with Humphry Repton, the celebrated landscape gardener, and through the patronage of the Prince Regent (later George IV). For his royal master, Nash designed Regent's Park, Regent Street and the Haymarket Theatre, remodelled

John Nash, bust outside his church of All Souls, Langham Place, London.

Cumberland Terrace, overlooking Regent's Park.

the Royal Pavilion in Brighton and renovated Buckingham Palace, building Marble Arch to stand at its entrance. Although willing to employ any architectural tradition, from Gothic to "Hindu", Nash is generally remembered for developing the neo-Classical style, which is known after his patron as "Regency".

NELSON,
Horatio (Viscount Nelson of the Nile & of Burnham Thorpe) (1758-1805)

The son of a Norfolk clergyman, Nelson joined the navy at 12 and had lost his right eye in action by the time he was 16. His distinguished service at the great battle of Cape St Vincent brought him to the rank of Rear Admiral in 1797, the year in which he lost an arm while attacking the Canary Islands. In 1798 he destroyed a French fleet at the battle of the Nile, thus ending Napoleon's attempt to conquer Egypt, and in 1801 he smashed the

The Battle of Trafalgar: "The Approach".

Vice-Admiral Lord Nelson, aged 43.

Danish fleet at Copenhagen, thus preventing the combined Baltic powers from joining the French against Britain. Promoted to supreme command in the Mediterranean, in 1803, Nelson blockaded the French base at Toulon for two years, then from January to October 1805 pursued Villeneuve's Franco-Spanish fleet to the West Indies and back, destroying it completely off Cape Trafalgar. This victory saved England from the immediate threat of a Napoleonic invasion and assured the nation world-wide naval supremacy for half a century.

A shy man of slight build, Nelson neverthe-less made himself conspicuous on the quarter-deck of his flagship, *Victory*, by appearing in full dress uniform, complete with his orders and decorations. Shot through the spine in his hour of triumph by a French sniper, Nelson was mourned by the nation and the navy as a gallant hero and a commander of genius. The novelist Joseph Conrad (1857-1924) later wrote of Nelson that "he brought heroism into the line of duty".

> "Rarely has a man been more favoured in the hour of his appearing, never one so fortunate in the moment of his death." (Admiral A. T. Mahan, *The Life of Nelson*)

NIGHTINGALE,
Florence
(1820-1910)

Florence Nightingale.

The creator of the modern nursing profession had a sheltered up-bringing in a wealthy home and had to fight against stiff parental opposition for the right to become a nurse. In 1851 she studied for three months at a Protestant hospital in Kaiserswerth, Germany, which had pioneered the training of nurses. In 1853 she became superintendent of a small hospital for women in London. The outbreak of the Crimean War (1854) led her, with forty volunteer nurses, to the hospital at Scutari where she imposed order and cleanli-

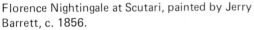

Florence Nightingale at Scutari, painted by Jerry Barrett, c. 1856.

ness on a hell of chaos and squalor and became a legend overnight. Within six months the fatality rate among the casualties fell from 42% to 2%. Public recognition of her work came in the form of subscriptions totalling £44,000 to a "Nightingale Fund", which she used to found the first British training school for nurses at St Thomas's Hospital, London. Within a decade practically every major hospital had at least one nurse trained in the methods of Miss Nightingale. A semi-invalid for most of her later life, she also helped to improve standards of child care in the home and of health in the peace-time army and in India. Thanks largely to her efforts, the first training course for health visitors was started in 1892. By her efforts and her example, Florence Nightingale not only revolutionized hospitals; she also raised the public's regard for women by making caring a profession.

> "The war in the East has not only exhibited the courage of English and French soldiers, but has also given rise to acts of the most sublime devotion on the part of the weaker sex.... Miss Nightingale possesses every advantage this world can afford. She is young, rich and in possession of a fortune ... she has, nevertheless, devoted herself to an existence of self-denial..." (*The Observer*, November 1854)

NORTHCLIFFE,
Lord (Alfred Charles William Harmsworth) (1865-1922)

One of the founding fathers of modern journalism, Northcliffe joined a newpaper on leaving school in 1880 and in 1883 founded the sensationalist magazine, *Answers*, which reached a weekly circulation of one million within four years. With the aid of his brother Harold (Lord Rothermere 1868-1940), he moved from periodicals into daily newspapers, with the *Evening News* (1894). In 1896 he launched the *Daily Mail*, which, at one half-penny, sold at half the price of most other newspapers. Within four years the *Mail*, too, had reached a daily circulation of one

Lord Northcliffe.

million. Northcliffe also founded the *Daily Mirror* (1903) and took over control of the *Observer* and the *Times*; but he continued to regard the *Daily Mail* as his most important publication. To boost its circulation still higher, he organized numerous publicity stunts such as air races, motor rallies and polar expeditions. During the Great War Northcliffe was put in charge of British propaganda to enemy countries. Northcliffe's methods were not universally admired. One critic said of the *Daily Mail* that it was written by office boys for office boys. Northcliffe himself is said to have told his staff to imagine that they were writing for a reader with a mental age of ten. The point is, however, that his formula was successful.

Frances Stevenson, Lloyd George's secretary, described him as "an extraordinarily commonplace man, with a very good brain for business . . . rather dull to talk to, very vain, but kind-hearted. . . . Nothing original." Beaverbrook called him "the greatest figure who ever strode down Fleet Street".

The *Daily Mail*.

NUFFIELD,
Viscount (William Richard Morris) (1877-1963)

Lord Nuffield did for Britain what Henry Ford did for America: he brought motoring to the millions, and by doing so became the country's largest single car manufacturer and a multi-millionaire. After an elementary education and a nine-month apprenticeship, he started work in a bicycle shop at the age of 16 and the following year set up in business for himself, repairing bicycles in a shed at

Lord Nuffield passing through a guard of honour on arrival at Guy's Hospital to lay the foundation stone of the new paying patients' block, 3 October 1934.

A Morris Cowley.

Cowley, near Oxford. From repairing he moved into manufacturing, first bicycles, then motor-bicycles and then motor cars (1912). After the Great War he introduced mass production methods and by 1926 was producing one thousand of his "Morris Cowley" models a week. At £165, they were well within the price-range of middle-class buyers. By 1939 he had produced over one million cars and had already begun to give large sums for charitable purposes and, in particular, to hospitals. In 1937 he founded Nuffield College, Oxford for research in the social sciences and in 1943 gave £10,000,000 to set up the Nuffield Foundation for research into medical, social and industrial problems. As a progressive employer, he was one of the first to introduce welfare schemes, paid holidays and sports facilities for his employees. In 1952 his own company and the Austin Company were merged to form the British Motor Corporation, the ancestor of British Leyland.

105

ORWELL,
George (Eric Blair)
(1903–50)

Born in India, but educated at Eton, Orwell served with the police in Burma (1922-27), where he developed an intense opposition to the system of privilege represented by British colonial rule. This view was powerfully expressed in his first novel, *Burmese Days* (1934). During the depression years of the 1930s Orwell drew on his personal experiences of poverty and the Spanish Civil War to write a series of documentary works — *Down and Out in Paris and London* (1933), *The Road to Wigan Pier* (1937) and *Homage to Catalonia* (1938). The rise to power of Stalin in Russia and Hitler in Germany filled Orwell with a deep hatred of totalitarian rule, which provided the theme for his best-known works, *Animal Farm* (1945) and *Nineteen Eighty Four* (1949).

George Orwell.

"To the ordinary working man . . . Socialism does not mean much more than better wages and shorter hours and nobody bossing you about." (*The Road to Wigan Pier*)

"If the war didn't happen to kill you it was bound to start you thinking." (*Coming Up for Air*)

"A family with wrong members in control — that, perhaps, is as near as one can come to describing England in a phrase. (*The Lion and the Unicorn*)

"The great enemy of clear language is insincerity." (*Politics and the English Language*)

OWEN,
Robert
(1771–1858)

A runaway at ten, a self-employed businessman at 14 and manager of a spinning-mill
with 500 employees at 20, Robert Owen is
remembered as a pioneer of personnel man-
agement, town planning, progressive education
and the theory and practice of socialism. At
New Lanark, near Glasgow he began to
implement his theory that, by improving the
living and working conditions of his employees,
he could improve their character and behaviour. Owen reduced the working day to
10½ hours, ended the employment of children

Robert Owen, by an unknown artist, 1851.

New Lanark.

under 10, opened a company shop to sell good products at low prices and provided free medical care and decent housing and opened a nursery school for infants. New Lanark and Owen's pamphlet, *A New View of Society*, in which he set out visionary schemes for future co-operative communities, won him an international reputation. His visitors included a future Tsar of Russia and the father of Queen Victoria. But Owen's criticisms of religion (1817) and his unconventional views on family life lost him support in influential circles. Nevertheless, he was successful in promoting the Factory Act of 1819, which tried to limit children's hours of work. In 1824 he founded a co-operative community at New Harmony in Indiana, but the venture failed and he lost £40,000 — four fifths of his fortune. Returning to England, he tried to set up a system of co-operatives to enable workers to exchange the goods they produced direct with one another without profit-taking middlemen. This scheme, too, proved a failure, as did his attempt to establish a Grand National Consolidated Trades Union (1834) as a sort of alternative government. He then founded a newspaper, *The New Moral World* (1834-41), to spread his views, but in his later years had little influence on public opinion.

PAINE,
Thomas
(1737-1809)

The son of a Norfolk farmer, Tom Paine lived in obscurity until 1772 when he lost his position as an excise officer for trying to organize a campaign for better wages. In 1774 he met Benjamin Franklin and decided to emigrate to America. Here the political crisis of the day provided the perfect subject for his talents as a radical pamphleteer, and in *Common Sense* (1776) and other writings he justified the American revolutionaries' struggle against British rule. Paine then served as a soldier in the revolutionary army and held several important posts in the American government before returning to England in

Thomas Paine, painted after an engraving of 1793.

Published as the Act directs by W. Locke Sept. 1791.

MAD TOM.
or the MAN of RIGHTS.

PALMERSTON,
Viscount (Henry John Temple)
(1784–1865)

Palmerston entered the House of Commons as a Tory in 1807 and two years later was appointed Secretary at War, an administrative post which he held for the next twenty years. Palmerston's early Conservatism weakened under the influence of the brilliant and liberal-minded Canning and in 1829 he joined the Whigs. In 1830 Palmerston became Foreign Secretary. His publicly stated policy was to

Palmerston, c.1860.

1787. In 1792 he fled to France to escape prosecution, following the publication of the second part of his *Rights of Man*, in which he defended the American and French revolutions and criticized the British system of government. Convicted of treason in his absence, he was received as a hero in France and elected a member of the revolutionary Convention. But he soon fell from favour for opposing the execution of Louis XVI and narrowly escaped being sent to the guillotine himself. In 1793 he published *The Age of Reason*, an attack on both Christianity and Atheism, written while he was in prison. This work did nothing to redeem him in the eyes of his countrymen and he returned to America (1802) where he died. Paine's democratic ideas remained an inspiration for British radicals throughout the nineteenth century.

NOW FOR IT!

A Set-to between "Pam, the Downing Street Pet," and "The Russian Spider."

Punch cartoon, 17 February 1855.

In his later years Palmerston's judgments were less sure — he over-rated the danger of a French invasion in the 1860s, sympathised with the Confederate South during the American Civil War and thought, wrongly, that he could bluff Bismarck out of taking Schleswig-Holstein. He was opposed to political and social reforms at home, but remained extremely popular in the country, if frequently the despair of his colleagues in Parliament. This was due in part to his policies, which seemed to be a no-nonsense assertion of British power, in part to his flamboyant personality and in part to his skilful handling of the press. Hard-working and physically tough, more prudent and less reckless than he seemed, Palmerston died aged 81, having held office for 48 years, 38 of them with Cabinet rank.

> "His administration at the Foreign Office was one long crime." (John Bright)
>
> ". . . A Conservative Minister working with Radical tools and keeping up a show of Liberalism in his foreign policy." (Lord Derby)
>
> "It was easy to settle affairs with Palmerston because he was a man of the world, and was therefore governed by the principle of honour." (Benjamin Disraeli)

preserve international peace in the interests of commerce, to make Britain's influence felt abroad and, where it did not conflict with either of the two previous objectives, to support national independence movements. In private, however, he would admit that it was desirable to bully the smaller powers from time to time. But his major initiatives, to settle disputes over Belgium and the Eastern Question, involved attempts to find a peaceful solution to potentially explosive problems by holding international conferences in London. During Palmerston's second spell at the Foreign Office (1846-51) he developed the arrogant style of "gun-boat diplomacy" usually associated with his name and the "Don Pacifico" incident (1850). Serving as Home Secretary from 1852 to 1855, he succeeded Aberdeen as Prime Minister (1855-58 and 1859-65), when it became clear that only he had the drive and energy to lead the war in the Crimea to a successful conclusion.

PANKHURST,
Mrs Emmeline
(1858-1928)

In 1889 Mrs Pankhurst, with her husband, Richard, a lawyer and supporter of women's rights, formed the Women's Franchise League to give women the vote. Her daughter,

Christabel (1880-1958), eventually persuaded her to form the more militant Women's Social and Political Union (1903). Negotiations with H. H. Asquith, the Liberal Prime Minister, convinced Mrs Pankhurst that his government would not pass legislation to give women the vote and that stronger measures were, therefore, necessary. As a result of her "direct action" tactics, Mrs Pankhurst was arrested on a number of occasions and, in protest, went on hunger strike. In 1913 she was imprisoned for three years on charges of directing a campaign of arson, but was released within a year. When war broke out in 1914, she threw her energies into mobilizing women for work in industry and in the armed

Mrs Pankhurst arrested outside Buckingham Palace, May 1914.

forces. When women over 30 finally got the vote in 1918, Mrs Pankhurst left the Independent Labour Party and migrated to Canada, where she worked on behalf of child welfare. Just before her death she was adopted as Conservative candidate for Whitechapel in London's East End. Her daughters, Christabel, Sylvia (1882-1960) and Adela (1885-1961) emigrated to North America, Ethiopia and Australia respectively, but remained devoted to the causes of socialism, pacifism and feminism.

A woman voter, 1918.

"We women suffragists have a great mission — the greatest mission the world has ever known. It is to free half the human race and through that freedom to save the rest." (Emmeline Pankhurst, Speech, October 1912)

PAXTON,
Joseph
(1803-65)

The designer of the "Crystal Palace", which housed the Great Exhibition of 1851, started his career as a gardener on the Duke of Devonshire's estate at Chatsworth. Having made a fortune from railway investments, Paxton travelled widely, designing parks, mansions and whole suburbs. His "Crystal Palace" — the name was invented by *Punch*, not the architect — was the largest building ever erected when it was put up, covering a

The Crystal Palace.

Joseph Paxton.

floor area of 772,284 square feet. It was later taken from its original site in Hyde Park and re-built in Sydenham, where it was finally destroyed by fire in 1936. A keen supporter of "sanitary reform", Paxton interested himself in many schemes for the improvement of London, including the building of an embankment along the Thames. One of his more visionary ideas was an eleven-mile glass roofed road to encircle the city. Knighted in 1851, Paxton served in Parliament from 1854 until his death, when the *Times* praised him as "the greatest gardener of his time, the founder of a new style of architecture and a man of genius who devoted it to objects in the highest and noblest sense popular".

PEEL,
Sir Robert
(1788-1850)

The son of Sir Robert Peel (1750-1830), a successful manufacturer and politician, Peel is best remembered as the founder of Britain's modern police system and as the man who, by repealing the Corn Laws, split the Tory Party for a generation. A cautious reformer, he recognized the need for change but opposed radical schemes. Entering the Commons in 1809, Peel held successive Cabinet posts until, as Home Secretary (1822-27, 1828-29), he reformed the criminal law, improved prison conditions and established the Metropolitan Police Force. An early opponent of Catholic Emancipation, he later helped to pass the Roman Catholic Relief Act (1829) when he

Sir Robert Peel, portrait by John Linnell, 1838.

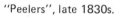

"Peelers", late 1830s.

became convinced that it was inevitable that Catholics should achieve the same civil and political rights as Protestants. Peel accepted the 1832 Reform Bill with similar reluctance, but did not oppose the Whig reforms of 1832-41 and in his "Tamworth Manifesto" (1834), an address to his electors, justified these changes in the constitution. Peel's own administration (1841-46) abolished import duties on raw materials and foodstuffs and passed important legislation to regulate joint-stock companies, railways, factory conditions and the Bank of England. The Irish famine of 1845-46 led Peel to repeal the Corn Laws, a tariff system which was intended to protect the interests of agricultural landowners. Because landowners were the mainstay of the Tory Party, many of Peel's followers, led by Disraeli, turned against him and he never held office again. He died after a fall in a riding accident. A hard-working administrator and a debater of great skill, Peel was much admired but not greatly liked. The Duke of Wellington once said "I have no small talk and Peel has no manners". Disraeli said that Peel had no life outside the House of Commons. That was both his strength and his weakness.

"In the administration of public affairs, as surely as a great act or measure is impracticable, you forthwith achieve it." (Harriet Martineau, Letter to Peel, February 1846)

PITT,
William (Pitt the Younger)
(1759-1806)

Born the younger son of the Earl of Chatham, Pitt became an MP at the age of 22, Chancellor of the Exchequer a year later and Prime Minister at the age of 24 — the youngest man ever to hold that high office. Between 1784 and 1802, when he resigned over George III's unwillingness to compromise on the question of Catholic Emancipation, Pitt carried through a wide range of reforms affecting the nation's system of tariffs and

William Pitt the Younger.

taxes (under the influence of Adam Smith), the government of India and Canada and the treatment of Catholics. He also supported William Wilberforce's campaign to abolish slavery. The outbreak of war with revolutionary France in 1793 turned Pitt's attention away from reform and led him to order repressive measures to suppress public disorder within Britain itself. After the Irish rising of 1798 he forced through the Act of Union, which created the United Kingdom of Great Britain and Ireland (1801). Pitt lacked his father's flair as a war-leader, and has been criticized for concentrating on overseas expeditions to the neglect of European operations; but during his second ministry (1804-6) he did negotiate the alliance with Russia and Austria which launched the war of the Third Coalition. Pitt's health was broken by the strain of long years in office and, though he lived long enough to see Nelson's victory at Trafalgar remove the shadow of the threat of invasion, he died soon after the news of Napoleon's victory at Austerlitz and the consequent collapse of the third alliance. A cold and clever man, Pitt was quite simply an extraordinarily able politician who loved power and used it with skill and integrity.

Pitt addressing the House of Commons on the French declaration of war, 1793, painted by Karl Anton Hickel.

PLACE, Francis (1771-1854)

Place is one of those historical figures whose significance has been exaggerated by historians because he provided them with so much material. When he died, he left behind some 70 volumes of his private papers and letters and a large collection of political pamphlets. Historians writing about the radical movements of the early nineteenth century have naturally been inclined to see Place as perhaps more the man of action than he actually was. A Londoner by birth, Place was apprenticed to a breeches-maker and in 1793 helped to organize a strike among his fellow workers. When the strike failed, Place was victimized and suffered eight months' unemployment. Determined to secure his own financial independence, so that he could pursue his political

Francis Place, portrait by Samuel Drummond, c.1830.

Presenting the Chartist petition of 1842.

PROCESSION ATTENDING THE GREAT NATIONAL PETITION OF 3,317,702, TO THE HOUSE OF COMMONS, 1842.

activities without fear of poverty, he set up in business as a tailor and became a successful small businessman. Within a few years the back room of his shop at Charing Cross had become a favoured meeting place for Radicals and Place himself an important committee man and back-room organizer. He worked for the election of the Radical, Sir Frances Burdett, who stood as a candidate for the Westminster constituency in 1807; he campaigned for the repeal of the Combination Acts against trade unions (1824) and in favour of parliamentary reform. He was a supporter of the penny post and helped to draft the People's Charter (1838), though he opposed Chartism, arguing that the working classes should accept middle-class radical leadership.

Place was strongly influenced in his thinking by Jeremy Bentham and tended to take a rather intellectual approach to politics. However revolutionary his ultimate aims, in practice, Place tended to support methods of gradual change through propaganda and legislation. A self-made, self-educated man, he was a firm believer in "self improvement" and never ceased to urge the working classes to follow his own example. He opposed Robert Owen's socialism and argued that competition, far from destroying relations between men, was "the greatest stimulus to improvement".

Place's death passed almost unnoticed and, had his biography not been written fifty years later by the eminent scholar, Graham Wallas, it is doubtful whether he would be remembered at all today, let alone figure as a major character in many text-book accounts of the Radical movement.

PUGIN,
Augustus Welby Northmore
(1812-52)

The son of a French artist, Pugin was a versatile and talented architect and designer, who worked on stage scenery, furniture, textiles, silver-ware, jewellery and, above all, stained glass. However, he is chiefly to be remembered as the leading spokesman of the "Gothic Revival", which transformed conventional English architecture — and thus so many of our cities and villages — in the nine-

A Pugin church in Gothic style.

Pugin, c. 1840, by an unknown artist.

teenth century. Converted to Roman Catholicism in 1835, Pugin argued in his book, *Contrasts* (1836), that medieval "Christian" styles had been produced by a healthier society and should therefore replace the "debased" Renaissance fashions then prevailing. The full title of Pugin's book reveals his viewpoint clearly — *Contrasts: or, a Parallel between the Noble Edifices of the Fourteenth and Fifteenth Centuries and Similar Buildings of the Present Day; shewing the Present Decay of Taste*. He returned to this argument in other books, such as his *True Principles of Pointed or Christian Architecture*, and in his plans for various houses and churches and his designs for the furniture and decorations of the rebuilt Houses of Parliament. The influence of his ideas spread not only to other architects but also into broader artistic circles, such as the Pre-Raphaelite Brotherhood which attracted William Morris and other socially-conscious artists of the day.

> ". . . this mania for paganism is developed in all classes of buildings erected since the fifteenth century . . . . The most celebrated palaces of Europe are the veriest heathen buildings imaginable . . . . The decoration . . . is invariably designed from heathen mythology . . . . In new Buckingham Palace . . . there is not even a regular chapel . . . both in appearance and arrangement it is utterly unsuited for a Christian residence." (A. W. N. Pugin, *Contrasts*)

REITH,
Lord
(1889-1971)

Trained as a civil engineer, Reith served in the army throughout the Great War. He then became involved in the development of radio and presided over the BBC during the crucial period of its development from 1922 to 1938. It was Reith's personal influence which was largely responsible for the establishment of the BBC's world-wide reputation for accuracy and impartiality. An austere man of the highest administrative ability, Reith served as the first chairman of BOAC, then successively as Minister of Information, Minister of Transport and Public Works and Chairman of the Commonwealth Telecommunications Board, the National Film Finance Corporation and the Colonial Development Corporation. Yet he never felt that he had found a job which really "stretched" him and engaged his capacities to the full. He is commemorated by the annual Reith Lectures, which were first broadcast in 1948.

Lord Reith addressing a conference for wireless group leaders in London, January 1932.

RHODES,
Cecil John
(1853–1902)

Cecil Rhodes was an adventurer whose main belief was that the English-speaking peoples had a mission to rule the world, and who devoted his life to forwarding that mission in Africa. Ill-health sent him at 17 to the sunny climate of Natal, from where he made his way to the diamond fields of Kimberley. Here he showed his genius for business dealing by amalgamating the various mining and trading companies to form the De Beers combine (1880), which gained a monopoly over production and sales and made Rhodes a millionaire. He also acquired a controlling interest in Consolidated Goldfields (1887) on the Witwatersrand. By this time he had undertaken several periods of study at Oxford and was turning his attention to politics. His ambition was to see the four South African provinces united under British rule and linked to Britain's other African colonies by a "Cape to Cairo" railway. The main obstacles to this policy were German expansionism and the Boer Republic of the Transvaal, governed by Paul Kruger. Rhodes blocked the Germans by getting southern Bechuanaland annexed to Cape Colony and the northern part taken over as a British protectorate. To the north and east of Bechuanaland lay vast territories, principally inhabited by the Matabele and Mashona peoples, which today form the

A cartoon from the *Westminster Gazette* captioned "The Kimberley Frog trying to make himself bigger than the Bull."

America, the Commonwealth and (until 1914) Germany, to study at Oxford. Rhodes' dream of a Cape to Cairo railway was never realized, but in 1910 a Union of South Africa was finally established. De Beers still controls the South African diamond industry and the Rhodes Scholarship scheme continues.

Cecil Rhodes, 1902.

states of Zimbabwe and Zambia. The British government refused Rhodes a protectorate but did give a charter (1889) to his British South Africa Company to develop and administer this area, which became known as Rhodesia. Rhodes ensured continuing British support for the venture by naming the first settlement in the region, Salisbury, after the Prime Minister of the day, believing that the British would never abandon any cause with which their prestige was so clearly associated. As Prime Minister of Cape Colony (1890), Rhodes attempted to support the Uitlanders (immigrants, mostly British) who were denied political rights in the Transvaal; but his involvement in the "Jameson Raid" (1895), an unsuccessful attempt to seize Johannesburg by force, led to his resignation (1896) and the end of his political career. In his will he left a large sum for "Rhodes Scholarships", to enable young men from

RUSKIN,
John
(1819–1900)

John Ruskin proclaimed that the only true wealth was beauty, at a time when the most influential of his countrymen seemed to believe that the only true beauty was wealth. As a boy he enjoyed a close relationship with

John Ruskin, portrait by Sir Hubert von Herkomer, 1879.

A cartoon of 1872.

his parents, travelled a great deal and showed an early talent for writing. A great admirer of Turner, he wrote an essay to defend his style against Turner's critics; this essay became a five-volume work on *Modern Painters*, the first volume being published when he was only 24. Apart from defending Turner, Ruskin called his readers to admire mountain scenery and Italian painting, especially that of Titian, and to reject everything in art that was insincere. The book was widely read and had considerable influence, especially on William Morris. Ruskin later championed the cause of the Pre-Raphaelite Brotherhood.

A study tour of Venice led Ruskin to write *Seven Lamps of Architecture* (1849) and *The Stones of Venice* (1851-53), in which he argued that a nation's character is revealed in the quality of its buildings.

Like William Morris, Ruskin turned from the study of art to the study of the society which produced it. In a collection of essays, *Unto this Last* (1862), he argued that men must be happy in their work to be able to produce artistic goods. In his later writings he developed this idea to suggest that useless work is immoral and that duties are more important than rights. An admirer of the medieval system of craft apprenticeship, Ruskin suggested the development of vocational schools. He also supported such advanced ideas as state-controlled industries, full employment, conservation and welfare services for the poor and aged.

In 1869 Ruskin was appointed as the first Slade Professor of Fine Art at Oxford but, despite his best efforts, failed to establish the study of art as a serious subject. From 1870 onwards he suffered from bouts of severe depression and mental illness. Much of his fortune was lost in attempts to promote craft work and art education. But his influence was much greater than his practical achievements.

RUSSELL,
Bertrand
(1872-1970)

The most eminent British philosopher in modern times, Bertrand Russell published several works of fundamental importance in the fields of logic and mathematics. He was, however, much concerned that the questions of philosophy should not remain matters of technical interest to philosophers alone. He was therefore passionately involved in the public issues of his times, writing and lecturing extensively on such matters as education, work and leisure and personal relationships. During the First World War his pacifism led him to be deprived of his Fellowship at

Bertrand Russell, portrait by Roger Fry, c.1923.

Bertrand Russell, aged 88, climbs to the base of Nelson's Column to speak in favour of nuclear disarmament.

Trinity College, Cambridge and to be imprisoned. However, his opposition to fascism led him to abandon his pacifism during the Second World War. But from 1949 onwards he began to campaign vigorously against atomic weapons and in 1956 he helped to found the Campaign for Nuclear Disarmament. His support for direct action tactics led to two months' imprisonment in 1961. In his last years he supported the protest movement against the war in Vietnam. In 1949 he was awarded the Order of Merit and in 1950 the Nobel Prize for Literature.

> "I think that bad philosophers may have a certain influence, good philosophers never." (Bertrand Russell, quoted in *The Observer*, April 1955)

SCOTT,
Robert Falcon
(1868-1912)

Scott's name stands for endurance. A professional sailor, born at Devonport, he was chosen to command a National Antarctic Expedition which from 1901 to 1904 discovered and named King Edward VII Land and organized expeditions into the interior of the Antarctic, penetrating further south than anyone had yet been. In 1910 he led a second expedition to reach the South Pole. After suffering terrible hardships, Scott and four companions reached the Pole on 18 January 1912, only to find a Norwegian flag there, showing that their rival, Amundsen, had beaten them by a month. Disastrous blizzards hindered the return journey and

Memorial statue, Portsmouth dockyard.

Scott and his two companions died of cold and starvation, after eight days without food, only eleven miles from the supplies at One Ton Camp. The bodies, together with Scott's moving diaries, were discovered by a search party eight months later. Scott's heroism made a deep impression on his countrymen and he was knighted in recognition of his valour.

Scott, 1911.

"For my own sake I do not regret this journey, which has shewn that Englishmen can endure hardships, help one another and meet death with as great a fortitude as ever in the past."
(R. F. Scott, Message to the Public, March 1912)

SCOTT,
Sir Walter
(1771-1832)

Born and educated in Edinburgh, Scott was trained for the law and practised in that profession throughout his life. His early interest in collecting and translating folk-ballads led him to compose original verse and with "The Lay of the Last Minstrel" (1805) he found fame. Overshadowed by Byron as a

Rob Roy separating a duel, from the 1867 edition of the novel.

Sir Walter Scott, portrait by Sir Edwin Landseer, c. 1824.

narrative poet, however, he refused the laureateship in 1813 and turned to fiction, producing, under the pen-name "Waverley", the celebrated historical romances for which he is now best known. They were an immediate success and have since attained the status of classics, some critics even claiming that Scott should be regarded as the "inventor" of the historical novel. They fall into two categories — those dealing with the recent history of Scotland, such as *The Heart of Midlothian* and *Rob Roy*, in which Scott was able to draw on personal knowledge and interviews with old people; and those, like *Ivanhoe* and *Quentin Durward*, which deal with the more remote past. The novels set in Scotland are the ones which seem to have endured the test of time rather better and they perhaps meant more to Scott himself, for he once wrote that his aim was to introduce Scots men and women "to those of the sister kingdom, in a more favourable light than they had been placed hitherto and tend to procure sympathies for their virtues and indulgence for their foibles".

Scott's enormous literary output also included biographies, histories and plays, but these were less successful than his poems and novels. A generous and open-hearted man, he lived in the style of a feudal laird on his estate at Abbotsford until the bankruptcy of the publishing firm with which he was associated plunged the partners deeply into debt (1826) and Scott killed himself with overwork, writing to pay off the debts which had been incurred during the days of his greatest success.

> ". . . a born story-teller: we can give him no higher praise . . ." (Henry James)
>
> ". . . a trivial mind and a heavy style . . ." (E. M. Forster)

SHAFTESBURY,
Lord (Anthony Ashley Cooper, 7th Earl) (1801-85)

A century after his death Shaftesbury's reputation remains untarnished. Few other "eminent Victorians" have fared so well. Shaftesbury himself would not have cared.

Shaftesbury.

because it is graphic, not only because it is true, but to show that the wretched condition of these children was just the same 15 years ago and upwards (we know not how long), previous to the establishment of the recent Commission.

The next species of employment to which children are put in the mines, as soon as they are strong enough, is that of dragging the loaded corves from the workings to the foot of the shaft. In some districts this is done by fixing a girdle round the naked waist, to which a chain from the corve is hooked and passed between the legs, and the boys or girls crawl on their hands and knees, drawing the corve full of coal after them. This is called "drawing by girdle and chain." In other districts the same kind of work is done by pushing with the head and hands from behind. This is called "putting," or "hurrying." Sometimes both the above methods are combined, as in the following illustration.

The printed evidence of the children, taken from various districts, will show the severe pain which this mode of labour inflicts. They attest that the girdle and chain frequently rub the skin off them, make blisters "as large as shillings and half-crowns," and otherwise injure the boys and girls. They get no rest all day, unless for a few moments at a time, and in general "only when something is the matter with the engine." The *human* engine, it will be perceived, is treated without any such consideration, though there is continually something the matter with it. The galling modes of work are various:—

Katharine Logan, 16 years old, coal-putter:—"Began to work at coal-carrying more than five years since; works in *harness* now; draws backwards, with face to the tubs; the ropes and chains go under pit-clothes; it is o'er sair work, especially when we crawl." (Franks, Report and Evidence, App. Pt. II., p. 389.)

But whence, it will be asked, do all these poor boys and girls bring their heavy loads of coal? From the remote darkness of a low, narrow den, in the bowels of the mine, at a distance from the shaft, perhaps, of upwards of 1000 yards, perhaps of 200, perhaps 2000, and through a passage of not more than from 18 to 20 inches in height. At the end of this there is the gloomy den called a "facing," a "heading," a "working," or a "man's room," and in that "room" lies the man at his work.

Rosa Lucas, aged 18, Lamberhead Green:—"Do you find it very hard work?—Yes, it is very hard work for a woman. I have been so tired many a time that I could scarcely wash myself. I could scarcely ever wash myself at night, I was Vol. I.

so tired; and I felt very dull and stiff when I set off in the morning." (Kennedy, Evidence, No. 92; App. Pt. II., p. 231, l. 53.)—James Crabtree, aged 15, Mr. Dearden's, near Todmorden:—Is it hard work for the lads in winter?—My brother falls asleep before his supper, and the little lass that helps him is often very tired." (Ibid. No. 71; p. 229, l. 17.)

—Peter Gaskell, Mr. Lancaster's, near Worsley:—"Has four sisters, and they have all worked in the pits; one of them works in the pits now; she sometimes complains of the severity of her work. Three years ago, when they had very hard work, I used to hear her complain of the *both* on her back, *and her legs were all eaten with the water*; she had to go through water to her work; she used to go about four or five o'clock in the morning, and stay till three or four in the afternoon, just as she was wanted; I have known her to be that tired at night that she would go to sleep before she had anything to eat." (Ibid. No. 29; p. 217, l. 36.)

North Lancashire Coal and Iron Mines.—Mr. Austin, after giving a deplorable picture of the labour of young children in the thin-seam mines, illustrates its effect by the words of the parents of some young workers. "I wish," one of them states, "you could see them come in; they come as tired as dogs, and throw themselves on the ground like dogs (here pointing to the hearthstone before the fire); we cannot get them to feed." (Austin, Report, ¶ 11; App. Pt. II., p. 807.)

It has been seen, that a foolish lord has been angry at the sketches given by the Commission, and declared them to be exaggerations, and so forth. The following extract will show that many more startling sketches might have been made. There are abundant instances; they were not illustrated; but are not the words pictures?

In this district (the West Riding of Yorkshire) girls are almost universally employed as trappers and hurriers in common

E

A page from an article in the *Illuminated Magazine*, 1844.

Driven by an aristocratic sense of duty and sustained by the keen conscience of an Evangelical Christian, he was swayed neither by persons nor parties.

Shaftesbury's first involvement in social problems was in the care of the insane; his first major triumph was the great Factory Act (1833) which regulated the working hours and conditions of children and appointed inspectors to enforce the law. In 1842, as a back-bench MP, he carried a Mines Act, which forbade the employment of females underground and again set limits on the labour of the young. Children were of special concern to him and he worked to improve their working conditions in agriculture, in brickyards and as chimney sweeps, as well as promoting "ragged schools" to give them the rudiments of an education. He also supported the abolition of slavery, the repeal of the Corn Laws, the public health movement and the early closing of shops. Believing in the force of example, he was a model employer and landlord. Despite his sympathy for the plight of the poor and the wretched, he remained staunchly Conservative in many of his views, opposing the first Reform Bill and trade unionism and strongly supporting strict observance of the Sabbath. He did much good and was willing to work with men of all political opinions, but his arrogance made him needless enemies. Respect rather than affection was his proper due, and that posterity has given him.

> "The [Anti Corn Law] League hate me as an aristocrat: the landowners as a Radical; the wealthy of all opinions, as a mover of inconvenient principles . . . . I have no political party . . . . Every class is against me . . ." (Diary, October 1845)
>
> ---
>
> "Lord Shaftesbury would have been in a lunatic asylum if he had not devoted himself to reforming lunatic asylums." (Florence Nightingale)

SHAW,
George Bernard
(1856–1950)

Shaw was an Irishman who became an English national institution. Even more remarkable, he made the theatre-going public think. Born into a poor Dublin household, the son of a drunken father and a music-loving mother, he worked in a series of dull office jobs before

Scenes from the first production of *Pygmalion* at His Majesty's Theatre, London, April 1914. Eliza Doolittle was played by Mrs Patrick Campbell and Henry Higgins by Sir Herbert Tree.

establishing himself in London as a critic, successively of books, art and music. Overcoming an early shyness to become a powerful and frequent public speaker, Shaw also became a strict vegetarian and a prominent member of the Fabian Society.

The first of his nearly fifty plays to reach the stage successfully — *The Devil's Disciple* — was performed in New York in 1897. Famous in Germany and America before he was known in Britain, Shaw had to wait until 1904 before one of his plays was put on in London's West End. Within ten years such works as *Man and Superman* (1903), *John Bull's Other Island* (1904) and *Major Barbara* (1905) had established him as a leading dramatist. In 1925 Shaw received the Nobel Prize for Literature. In his plays, and in such prose works as *The Intelligent Woman's Guide*

to Socialism and Capitalism (1928), he attacked hypocrisy and social injustice. An effective broadcaster from the early days of radio, Shaw earned a second bout of public acclaim when his plays began to be filmed in the 1930s. Provocative and cantankerous, he enjoyed fame as much as he deserved it.

"I am of the true Shakespearian type. I understand everything and everyone and am nobody and nothing." (Shaw on himself, 1930)

"He hasn't an enemy in the world and none of his friends like him." (Oscar Wilde)

George Bernard Shaw.

SMITH,
Adam
(1723-90)

Adam Smith was the founder of the modern study of economics. His *Enquiry into the Nature and Causes of the Wealth of Nations* (1776) is regarded as the classic statement of the doctrine of "laissez-faire" — the belief that governments should interfere as little as possible in economic affairs because, left to themselves, private individuals know best how to pursue their own interests and, in doing so, promote the interests of the community as a whole. William Pitt praised Smith's work and prophesied that it would shape the economic policies of succeeding generations. It did.

Adam Smith.

A view of Portsmouth — private enterprise in action.

STANLEY,
Henry Morton
(1841-1904)

Had he never become famous as "the man who found Livingstone", Stanley would still be celebrated as the most adventurous journalist of his day. Born John Rowlands and brought up in a Welsh workhouse, he ran away to sea, was adopted by a New Orleans merchant, whose name he took, and became an American citizen. After volunteering for

A signed drawing of Stanley by Lehmann, 1890.

Henry M Stanley

Oct 18ᵗʰ 1890

MR. STANLEY,
IN THE DRESS HE WORE WHEN HE MET DR. LIVINGSTONE IN AFRICA.

the Confederate army, he changed sides to serve in the artillery and then the navy on the Union side. Seeking adventure, he made his way to Asia Minor, was shipwrecked off the coast of Spain and eventually made a reputation as a journalist by serving as a war correspondent, first with Hancock, fighting Sioux Indians, and then with Napier in Abyssinia. By leading a column to find Livingstone in Central Africa (1871), Stanley then pulled off the scoop of the century. After that, he became an explorer in his own right and traced the entire course of the Congo river (1874-77), thus opening the heart of Africa to European trade and missionary enterprise. In 1879 he returned to Africa in the service of Leopold II of Belgium to organize the Congo Free State (1879-84). His last great journey was undertaken to "rescue" Emin Pasha, a former lieutenant of General Gordon, who had been abandoned with his Egyptian troops when the Mahdi conquered the Sudan. The expedition was dogged by confusion and tragedy, but Stanley returned to Britain a hero nonetheless, married a society beauty in Westminster Abbey, was re-naturalized a British subject, elected to Parliament (1895-1900) and created a Knight of the Bath. A popular lecturer in three continents, Stanley was also an extremely successful author. His major publications, *How I found Livingstone* (1872), *Through the Dark Continent* (1878) and *In Darkest Africa* (1890), enjoyed immense sales and, no doubt, contributed powerfully to establishing European stereotypes of Africans as vicious, treacherous or incompetent. Stanley's experiences of African peoples were, however, largely a reflection of his own arrogant and suspicious manner and of a piece with the harsh treatment he handed out to all who delayed or opposed him. A man with an iron constitution and an iron will, Stanley was a hero unredeemed by any concern for others. The people of the Congo called him "Bula Matari" — the breaker of rocks — and he is perhaps better remembered for his incredible energy than for the purposes he used it to achieve.

STEPHENSON,
George
(1781–1848)

The father of modern railways was the self-taught son of a pit fireman. Fascinated by machinery from childhood, he went to night school in his late teens so that he could read the works of James Watt. By 1815 he was enough of a technologist to devise a miner's safety lamp which won him an award of a thousand pounds. But he was already engaged

A working-class-man's magazine of 1859.

on a larger project, the perfection of a locomotive (self-moving) steam-engine. He drew
on the work of other pioneers, such as
Richard Trevithick (1771-1833), and added
major improvements of his own, notably the
multi-tubular boiler and the use of flanged
wheels. In 1821 Stephenson began work on
building the Stockton and Darlington Railway, a freight line which opened in 1825 and
was an immediate success. Stephenson's
masterpiece, however, was the Liverpool and
Manchester Railway (built 1826-30), recognized by contemporaries as the greatest
engineering feat since the building of the
pyramids. This also employed locomotives
based on Stephenson's prize-winning *Rocket*
which had beaten all comers at the celebrated Rainhill trials in 1829. Stephenson
built many other railways before retiring in
1840. In 1847 he became the first President
of the Institute of Mechanical Engineers. His
son, Robert (1803-59), carried on his work
and became a notable builder of bridges.

STOPES,
Marie (Charlotte Carmichael)
(1880–1958)

The pioneer of birth-control in Britain first
achieved a public reputation as an academic
expert on fossil plants and the problems of
coal-mining. But the break-up of her first
marriage led her to an interest in the
emotional and sexual aspects of married
life. Unlike earlier advocates of contraception, Marie Stopes saw it less in economic
terms, as a means of reducing poverty and

With the staff of her Holloway Road clinic, 1921.

The locomotive "Planet".

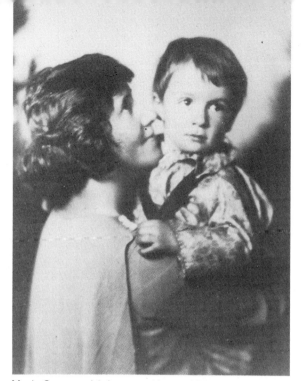

Marie Stopes with her son, Harry, 1926.

overpopulation, than in human terms, as a means of creating better relations between men and women. In 1918 she published *Married Love* and *Wise Parenthood*, the first books to make information about birth-control available to the general public in straightforward language. These books were widely translated and brought her a world-wide reputation. In 1921 Marie Stopes established the first birth-control clinic in the United Kingdom at Holloway in London. Her lectures, writings and practical work in the cause of contraception provoked much opposition, especially from Roman Catholics, but her influence in changing public attitudes on this subject was profound.

"Hitherto contraception had been practised as if it were a sort of secret vice but now it came into open discussion. A prophet was found to conduct this difficult campaign with religious fervour, no sense of humour and complete integrity — Dr. Marie Stopes." (Robert Graves and Alan Hodge, *The Long Week-End*)

TELFORD,
Thomas
(1757-1834)

When Telford was born, civil engineering was still a craft. When he died, it was a profession and Telford himself was largely responsible for this change. The son of a Dumfriesshire shepherd, Telford was apprenticed to a stone-mason at the age of 14. After working in Edinburgh and London, he became a surveyor of public works for Shropshire (1786), where he built bridges over the river Severn, including the iron bridge at Buildwas. He made his reputation, however, with the Ellesmere Canal (1793), which connected the Severn, the Mersey and the Dee. In 1801 the government commissioned him to make a naval defence survey of Scottish ports and harbours, which led him to undertake many improvements in their facilities. In 1804 he was put in charge of the construction of the Caledonian Canal, which ran from sea to sea through the Highlands. (The first vessel passed through it in 1822.) He also planned (1808-10)

Thomas Telford.

The Menai Bridge.

the Swedish Gotha Canal between the Baltic and the North Sea. Telford also built more than 1,000 miles of roads, pioneering a new technique which used a firmly packed bed of hand-picked stones, which would not be washed away or broken up by frost or traffic. Although most of his roads are in Scotland, his most famous one runs through North Wales, from Shrewsbury to Holyhead and Anglesey, crossing his famous Menai suspension bridge. In 1818 he founded and became first President of the Institute of Civil Engineers.

TURNER,
J. M. W.
(1775-1851)

Joseph Mallard William Turner was born in a squalid slum, the son of a Covent Garden barber. Rejected by his first employer as lacking in talent, he became the foremost landscape artist of the nineteenth century. His extraordinary ability enabled him to achieve fame and prosperity while still a young man.

J. M. W. Turner, by Charles Turner, 1842.

His first picture was exhibited at the Royal Academy while he was still only 15, and he was elected RA by the time he was 27. His early reputation was built on his facility in producing grand imitations of traditional themes, but his lasting fame rests in the remarkable pictures he produced as a mature artist in his sixties — *The Fighting Temeraire, The Snowstorm, The Approach to Venice* and *Rain, Steam and Speed*. A water-colour artist of unrivalled genius, Turner was obsessed with the reproduction of light, a problem to which he devoted years of study and research. Although his enthusiasm for his work estab-lished his permanent reputation, he left no school of devoted followers and it was left to the French Impressionists to exploit the break-through he had made, though Ruskin saw and proclaimed the importance of his work. Turner bequeathed to the nation some 300 of his paintings and more than 20,000 of his drawings and water-colour sketches. Most of these are housed in the Tate Gallery, London.

The Fighting Temeraire.

VICTORIA,
Queen
(1819-1901)

To posterity the very symbol of respectability, Victoria was in her own day a surprisingly controversial figure. When she came to the throne (1837), the popularity of the monarchy was at a low ebb. She vowed "I will be good", but had little understanding of the duties of a constitutional monarch and gave her confidence so completely to Lord Melbourne, the Whig leader, that Peel refused to form a government (1839) because he believed her sympathies were so much against his party. After her marriage to her cousin, Prince Albert of Saxe-Coburg-Gotha (1819-61), she tried to follow his ideal of the impartial sovereign. Utterly devoted to her husband, by whom she had nine children, she was stricken by his death and virtually retired from public life, forfeiting much of the popularity which had been gained by her happy family life. As the Queen grew older, however, her ceremonial role made her a venerated national figure. A warm admirer of Disraeli, Victoria failed to appreciate either Gladstone's loyalty or his virtues. She also continued to try to use her personal influence in foreign affairs and over appointments in the Church and the armed forces. Despite her popularity, Victoria was

The young Victoria.

hostile to many of the trends of her times, mistrusting the growth of democracy and condemning the movement for women's rights as "mad, wicked folly". Her Golden (1887) and Diamond (1897) Jubilees were, however, occasions for great national rejoicing.

"The golden reign is closed. The supreme woman of the world, best of the highest, greatest of the good, is gone. The Victorian age is over. Never, never was loss like this, so inward and profound that only the slow years can reveal its true reality. The Queen is dead." (*Daily Telegraph*, January 1901)

Victoria at Osborne, with her servant John Brown, painted by Sir Edwin Landseer.

WATT,
James
(1736-1819)

Greenock-born James Watt did *not* invent the steam-engine, but he did so improve it as to make it a practical source of power for such a wide range of processes that the general mechanization of manufacture was enabled to take place on a scale and at a pace previously impossible. Before Watt, the "beam-engines" of Thomas Newcomen (1663-1729) were generally used only for pumping water out of mines.

James Watt, aged 57, an engraving by S. W. Reynolds.

Watt's workshop.

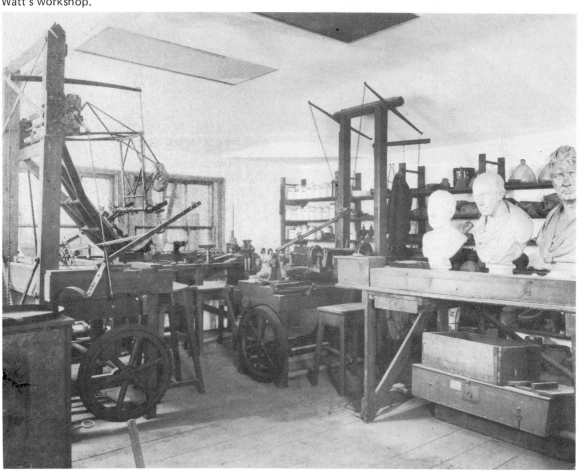

Trained in London as a maker of mathematical instruments, Watt worked as a technician at Glasgow University until, after repairing a model of a Newcomen engine, he invented the separate condenser (1765), a modification which greatly improved standards of heat-efficiency. In 1774 Watt went into partnership with Matthew Boulton, a successful Birmingham manufacturer, who was able to support Watt's further experiments by supplying the necessary cash and technical help. Perseverance led to prosperity as the partners' engines proved their worth and Watt improved them still further by adapting them to provide rotary motion and by inventing the centrifugal governor to regulate their speed. This device has been regarded as the world's first example of automation. By 1800 some five hundred Watt engines were at work. Elected a Fellow of the Royal Society in 1785, Watt also invented a document-copying machine, steam-powered coin-presses for the Royal Mint and a machine for copying sculpture. He also invented the idea of measuring the output of engines in "horse-power". The equivalent unit of power in the metric system is called a "watt" in his honour. Unlike most inventors of his day, Watt died famous, wealthy and respected.

WEBB,
Beatrice (1858-1943) and Sidney James (Lord Passfield) (1859-1947)

Sidney and Beatrice Webb were probably the most influential socialists of their times, not in the sense of building up the Labour Party as an organization or fighting for the cause in elections, but in the sense that their theories defined what socialism ought to mean in practice; and their theories were eminently practical ones. Sidney, a brilliant civil servant, and his wife Beatrice, a wealthy heiress who had devoted herself to social work, were both

Sidney & Beatrice Webb

prominent founder members of the Fabian Society (1884), which was dedicated to reform through step-by-step measures — the "inevitability of gradualness", in Sidney's phrase — rather than through violent revolution. In 1892 Sidney was elected to the newly-established London County Council and took a leading part in developing technical education. In 1894 he helped to found the London School of Economics. In 1895 Beatrice was appointed a member of a Royal Commission on the Poor Law and was responsible for the famous "Minority Report" (1909), which called, unsuccessfully, for its complete abolition. Just before the outbreak of the Great War, they jointly founded the weekly political journal, the *New Statesman*. In 1922 Sidney became an MP and served as a Minister in both inter-war Labour Governments. In 1929 he accepted the title of Lord Passfield; Beatrice disapproved and refused to use it. After a tour of Russia they published their last major work, *Soviet Communism: A New Civilization?* (1935), which gave an idealized view of Soviet Russia. Beatrice Webb's diaries, however, provide a perceptive and frank commentary on the events of her life-time and their *History of Trade Unionism* remains a classic work on its subject.

WEDGWOOD,
Josiah
(1730-95)

Gladstone said of Wedgwood that he was "the greatest man who ever . . . applied himself to the important work of uniting art with industry". Certainly this son of an obscure Staffordshire potter made his name a household word in his own lifetime and created a firm whose products are renowned world-wide to this day. A keen student of technology, Wedgwood was himself responsible for patenting a number of inventions, including the pyrometer, a device for measuring high temperatures. He was also a prominent member of the Lunar Society, which met in Birmingham each month to discuss scientific matters. As a practical businessman he was an energetic promoter of improved roads and canals. But he was also sensitive to the artistic aspects of his craft, showing an eager interest in the fashion for classical models which followed the excavation of Pompeii, and employing the talented John Flaxman (1755-1826) as one of his designers. Before all things, however,

Etruria, a model factory.

Wedgwood was a superb salesman. His wares were as good as those of his rivals, but not vastly superior. He took advantage of techniques of mass-production, but never tried to cut his prices. Rather by producing special wares for royal and aristocratic patrons did he make his name a by-word for quality and style. Wedgwood gave his customers what he made them want. A Radical in politics and a dissenter in religion, Wedgwood was also a strong supporter of both the American Revolution and the anti-slavery movement.

Wedgwood, seated, with his family in the grounds of his home, Etruria Hall, Staffordshire, painted by George Stubbs, 1780.

WELLINGTON,
Duke of (Arthur Wellesley)
(1769–1852)

England's most successful general between Marlborough and Montgomery, Wellington never lost a battle. He held his first major command in India, where he crushed the Maratha Confederacy (1803), but he made his reputation in the long struggle of the Peninsular War (1808-14), where his experience of fighting with irregular troops in wild country proved invaluable. His skilful fortification of the lines of Torres Vedras (1810) saved Lisbon from being overrun by the French, and his victory at Vittoria (1813) drove them out of Spain altogether. Criticized for his caution, Wellington never forgot that he was commanding England's only army

An engraving of 1817.

Wellington, portrait by Sir Thomas Lawrence, 1814.

BATTLE OF WATERLOO.
RETREAT OF THE FRENCH PURSUED BY ENGLISH CAVALRY AND INFANTRY

against some of Napoleon's most brilliant generals. At Waterloo (1815) Wellington met Napoleon in battle for the first and only time and defeated him. This decisive conflict, which ended more than two decades of war, was, in Wellington's own phrase, "a damned close run thing", but it made him a national hero for a generation.

The qualities of determination and diligence which served the "Iron Duke" so well in war were of less value to him in politics, where his blunt manner often embarrassed and irritated his colleagues. Wellington's involvement in government was less a matter of inclination than of duty; accustomed to command, he had little ability to persuade. As Prime Minister (1828-30), he opposed the reform of parliament, but after 1832 accepted both this and the repeal of the Corn Laws (1846). As Commander-in-Chief, he opposed changes which might have enabled the army to make a better showing in the Crimean War (1854-56). His funeral was an occasion of unparalleled national mourning.

"The Duke's government — a dictatorship of patriotism." (Benjamin Disraeli)

"He was the GREATEST man this country ever produced, and the most *devoted* and *loyal* subject, and the staunchest supporter the Crown ever had. . . ." (Queen Victoria)

"I like to walk alone." (Wellington on himself, 1801)

WELLS, H. G. (1866-1946)

H. G. Wells knew a great deal about science and even more about ordinary people. In his short stories and novels, and later in his educational writings, Wells tried to explain to a mass readership how science was revolutionizing their lives. In his old age he became increasingly convinced that "human history becomes more and more a race between education and catastrophe".

H. G. Wells.

such innovations as aerial and tank warfare and the atomic bomb and gained a reputation as a prophet of *Things to Come* (the title of one of his later works, an anti-war fantasy); but he also wrote convincingly, in such works as *Kipps* (1905) and *The History of Mr Polly* (1910), about the dreams and problems of working men and women.

Believing that science and education could lead to the creation of a peaceful "World State", Wells devoted his later years to popularizing academic knowledge in such works as *The Outline of History* (1920) and *The Science of Life* (1931). Depressed and frustrated by the political conflicts of his times, Wells yet exercised an immense influence on popular thinking, for he remained a visionary with the common touch.

"Whatever Wells writes is not only alive, but kicking." (Henry James)

". . . it was a wonderful experience for a boy to discover H. G. Wells . . . this wonderful man . . . who *knew* that the future was not going to be what respectable people imagined." (George Orwell)

H. G. Wells, by Claud Lovat Fraser, inscribed "Mr H. G. Wells penetrates the unknown".

The son of an unsuccessful tradesman and professional cricketer, Wells in his early life struggled hard against poverty to gain an education. This early struggle later made him a socialist and an early member of the Fabian Society. Successively apprenticed to a chemist and a draper, Wells eventually became a teacher and gained a university science degree before the success of his science fiction stories, beginning with *The Time Machine* (1895), made it possible for him to devote himself full-time to writing. Wells predicted

WESLEY,
John
(1703-91)

Wesley preaching *outside* a church.

The founder of Methodism was the fifteenth child of an Anglican clergyman. At Oxford he and his younger brother, Charles (1707-88), founded the Holy Club, a group of young men devoted to the study of the Bible and the strict observance of religious rituals and rules. The regularity of their devotions won them the nick-name of "Methodists". After failing as a missionary in the new American colony of Georgia (1735-37), Wesley experienced a renewal of his faith at a Moravian gospel meeting in Aldersgate Street, London. Convinced of his mission,

John Wesley, portrait by Nathaniel Hone, c. 1766.

Wesley devoted the rest of his long life to proclaiming the gospel, riding some 4,000 miles a year and preaching some 40,000 sermons. In his journal he declared that "I look upon all the world as my parish". Many of the Church of England clergy were made uncomfortable by his fervour, but Wesley was no more deterred by them than by the jeering mobs who broke up his meetings. A believer in organization and discipline, Wesley gradually came to the conclusion that, because Anglican clergy sometimes refused the sacraments to Methodists, there would have to be a separate Methodist Church. He therefore assumed the powers of a bishop (1784) and ordained ministers, some of whom went to America to lead the Methodist movement there. The author of numerous books and hymns, Wesley did more to revive religious life in England than any other man of his times.

WILBERFORCE, William (1759-1833)

Remembered chiefly for his campaign against slavery, Wilberforce entered Parliament at the age of 21, a wealthy heir, a gambler and man about town, and the close friend of William

William Wilberforce, portrait by Sir Thomas Lawrence, 1828.

Pitt, a companion from Cambridge days. Converted to Evangelical Christianity in 1784, Wilberforce renounced his former way of life, and in the course of time became a leading member of the influential "Clapham Sect", a group of Christians earnestly devoted to the cause of moral reform. In 1787 Wilberforce recorded in his journal "God Almighty has placed before me two great objects, the suppression of the slave trade and the reformation of manners", and in the same year he began, with Pitt's support, to crusade for the abolition of slave-trading. Despite many setbacks, he continued his efforts to turn the attention of Parliament to this issue in the face of the distractions of the country's wars

WILKES,
John
(1727-97)

Wilkes was not so much a politician as a political celebrity, a controversial figure renowned for what he stood for rather than for what he did. Entering Parliament at the age of 30, he used his periodical, the *North Briton*, to attack the speech made by George III at the opening of Parliament in 1763. The King ordered the issue of a general warrant for the arrest of Wilkes and 48 other persons.

Wilkes, by Richard Earlom.

against France. Finally, in 1807, a bill to abolish the slave trade was passed. The abolition of slavery itself was not, however, achieved until the year of Wilberforce's death, long after he had retired from Parliament (1824). It must also be emphasized that, while Wilberforce led the campaign in Parliament, many other reformers, such as Thomas Clarkson (1760-1846), made equally important contributions to the abolitionist movement. Frail in health, but strengthened by his religious convictions, Wilberforce gave away much of his fortune to charity and in his youth was also a supporter of parliamentary and factory reform. He also founded the Church Missionary Society and the Bible Society. As he grew older, he became more Conservative in his views, placing more emphasis on religion than reform.

Wilkes and Liberty! drawn by Hogarth, 1763.

being repeatedly re-elected to Parliament and repeatedly being expelled. To the cry of "Wilkes and Liberty", his right to enter the Commons, and thus the right of the Middlesex electors to choose their own Member without interference, was at last confirmed. Wilkes later established the right of the press to report parliamentary debates (1771) and, as Lord Mayor of London (1774), struggled to uphold the traditional rights of the City. A bold supporter of rights in general, he did little to advance any particular reforms and lost popularity by standing against the mob during the anti-Catholic Gordon riots (1780). His chief importance lies in the fact that he showed that public opinion, however crudely expressed, could not be ignored in the conduct of the nation's affairs.

"I scarcely ever met with a better companion, he has inexhaustible spirits, infinite wit and humour and a great deal of knowledge; but . . . his life is stained with every vice, and his conversation full of blasphemy and indecency. These morals he glories in; for shame is a weakness he has long since surmounted." (Edward Gibbon)

Released after a week, Wilkes protested against his arrest and went to court to establish a fundamental principle of British liberty, the judge ruling against the Crown's argument that it had acted "of State necessity" and stating flatly that "public policy was not an argument in a court of law". This judgment ended general warrants for good. A warrant for arrest can only be issued when a specific person is charged with a specific offence. Wilkes, despite this victory, was still judged to have been guilty of seditious libel. He fled to Paris and, in his absence, was sentenced to imprisonment and expelled from Parliament. In 1769 he tried to get back into the Commons, and was triumphantly elected as Member for Middlesex, only to be imprisoned for his libel offence. Months of mass demonstrations followed, with Wilkes

Places to Visit

Adam

London has many examples of Adam's work, including Apsley House (Hyde Park Corner, London W1), Osterley (Middlesex), Kenwood (Hampstead Lane, London NW3) and the interior of Syon House, Isleworth. Other fine examples of his work include Pulteney Bridge (Bath), Culzean Castle (Strathclyde), the General Register House (Edinburgh), Yester House (Gifford, Lothian), the church of St Andrew (Gunton, Norfolk) and the interiors of Harewood House (W. Yorks), Headfort House (Meath), Kedleston Hall (Derbyshire), Mellerstain House (Borders) and Saltram House (Devon).

Aspley House, with the statue of Wellington nearby.

Albert

The Albert Memorial (Kensington Gore, London SW7) shows the Prince, beneath an ornate canopy, holding a catalogue of the Great Exhibition. The base of the Memorial is covered with sculptures depicting scenes of industry and the empire and great men of culture. Opposite stands the Albert Hall. At Windsor can be seen the Albert Memorial Chapel, and at nearby Frogmore the Royal Mausoleum where Albert is buried.

Austen

Jane Austen's home at Chawton (Hants) is now a museum, containing many of her personal possessions.

Baird

The story of television is graphically represented at the IBA Broadcasting Gallery (70 Brompton Rd, London SW3). The exhibits include a replica of the TV camera which Baird demonstrated in 1926.

Banks

Banks' large botanical exhibition can now be seen among the exhibits of the Natural History Museum, Kensington. Kew Gardens, Richmond also owe much to his efforts.

Booth (William)

The Salvation Army Museum (Judd St, London WC1) contains many items associated with Booth as well as telling the story of the movement he founded.

Brown

Capability Brown's gardens can still be seen at Syon Park (Isleworth), Chatsworth (Derbyshire) and Burton Constable (Humberside). At Claremont (Surrey) there is a mansion, now a girls' school, designed by Brown for Clive of India.

Brunel

Brunel's great achievement, the Great Western Railway, has its own museum at Swindon. His surviving works include the Clifton Suspension Bridge (Bristol), completed only after his death, the nearby *SS Great Britain* and the Royal Albert Bridge (Saltash, Cornwall).

Byron
Byron's family homes, Newstead Abbey and Thrumpton Hall (Notts), contain many relics of the poet.

Churchill
Churchill's country home, Chartwell (near Westerham, Kent), has been preserved as a memorial to him. The Cabinet War rooms, beneath Whitehall, the nerve centre from which Churchill directed operations, can also be visited. At Blenheim Palace (Oxfordshire) the room in which he was born can be seen. At nearby Bladon lies his grave.

The birthplace of Charles Dickens in Portsmouth.

Constable
Outstanding examples of Constable's work are to be found in the Victoria and Albert Museum, the National Gallery and the Tate Gallery. His grave lies in the church of St John's, Hampstead.

Cook
There is a gallery devoted to Captain Cook in the National Maritime Museum (Greenwich, London SE10). Among the exhibits are his navigational instruments and a model of the *Endeavour*.

Darwin
Down House (Downe, Greater London) was Darwin's home for 40 years and now contains relics of the great man and other scientists.

Dickens
Dickens' house at 48 Doughty St (London WC1) is now a museum with a reconstruction of the kitchen at Dingly Dell, described in the *Pickwick Papers*, in the basement. His birthplace, 39a Commercial Road, Portsmouth, is also a museum devoted to his memory. At Broadstairs (Kent) Fort House (the model for Bleak House), where the author wrote *David Copperfield*, can also be seen. Other Dickens' relics can be seen in the local museum at Rochester (Kent), another area with which the author was long connected.

Disraeli
Hughenden Manor (near High Wycombe, Bucks) was Disraeli's home from 1847 and is now a museum devoted to his memory.

Edward VII
Edward VII's London home, Marlborough House, the scene of many glittering receptions and focus of the "Marlborough House Set" can still be visited.

Faraday
Some of Faraday's early scientific instruments can be seen at the Cuming Museum (Walworth Road, London SE17), but his major monument is his laboratory, preserved in the basement of the Royal Institution (21 Albe-

marle St, London W1), where it forms the centrepiece of a museum devoted to his life and work.

Grace
Lord's Cricket Museum at the Lord's Ground, London NW8 contains many sketches and mementoes of W. G. Grace, including the ball with which he scored his 100th century in 1895.

Hill
Sir Rowland Hill's statue stands outside the National Postal Museum (King Edward St, London EC1), which houses one of the world's greatest collections of stamps – some 250,000 in all, including every British stamp issued since 1840. Hill's house is now the Bruce Castle Museum (Lordship Lane, Tottenham, London N17), which contains an extensive collection of postal relics.

Hogarth
Hogarth's work can be seen in the National Gallery, the Tate Gallery and the Thomas Coram Foundation for Children (40 Brunswick Sq, London WC1). His house (Hogarth Lane, Great West Road, Chiswick, London W4) contains paintings, prints and relics associated with the artist.

Dr Johnson's house.

Johnson
Dr Johnson wrote his famous dictionary at 17 Gough Square, London EC4 and the house is now preserved as a museum. Nearby is the Cheshire Cheese, his favourite inn. Johnson's birthplace in Lichfield (Staffs) is also a museum.

Kipling
Kipling's house, "Bateman's" at Burwash (Sussex), contains many of his personal possessions and is surrounded by a garden he laid out himself.

Lloyd George
The Lloyd George Memorial Museum is built in the grounds of the house in which he died, Ty Newydd, in the village of Llanystumdwy, where he spent his childhood.

Montgomery
Montgomery's motorized campaign caravans can now be seen at the Imperial War Museum (Lambeth Road, London SE1).

Morris
The William Morris Gallery (at Lloyd Park, Forest Road, Walthamstow, London E17) is devoted to the artist's life and work. Room 119 at the Victoria and Albert Museum also shows a selection of his work. Kelmscott Manor (Oxfordshire), Morris's summer home from 1871 to 1896, can be visited by arrangement. Morris was also responsible for the interior decorations of Wightwick Manor,

Staffs. Examples of his stained glass can be seen at the following churches – St Nicholas (Bromham, Wilts), St Mary (Nun Monkton, N. Yorks), St Denys (Rotherfield, E. Sussex) and St Editha (Tamworth, Staffs).

Mountbatten
A special room at the Imperial War Museum (Lambeth Road, London SE1) commemorates the Mountbatten family.

Nash
London is especially rich in Nash's work. Outstanding examples are Carlton House Terrace, Clarence House, Regent's Park, the Royal Mews at Buckingham Palace, the Theatre Royal, Haymarket, All Souls Church in Langham Place and the Rotunda, Repository Road, Woolwich. Much is also to be seen in Ireland, including the Protestant church at Caher (Tipperary), Killymoon Castle (Tyrone), Lissan Rectory (Tyrone), Lough Cutra Castle (Galway) and the green house at Shane's Castle (Antrim). The most celebrated of all Nash's creations is perhaps the Royal Pavilion at Brighton, described by one expert as "the most fantastic palace in Europe". Other Nash projects include the ten different projects at Blaise Hamlet (Avon) and the Town Hall at Newport (Isle of Wight).

Nelson
There is a gallery devoted to Nelson in the National Maritime Museum (Greenwich, London SE10). Madame Tussaud's (Marylebone Rd, London NW1) contains a tableau representing the lower gun-deck of the *Victory* at the Battle of Trafalgar. The ship itself can still be visited at Portsmouth. Opposite Nelson's flagship stands the Royal Naval Museum with many relics of the admiral, models of ships of his time and a panorama of the Battle of Trafalgar.

Nightingale
Florence Nightingale's awards and jewellery can be seen at the National Army Museum (Royal Hospital Road, Chelsea).

The *Victory*, Portsmouth.

Owen
Owen's model factory and village settlement at New Lanark (Strathclyde) can still be seen and an exhibition charts the progress of their restoration. At Newtown, Powys, in a building which was once his home, is a Memorial Museum housing books, pictures and personal relics.

Paine
A first edition of the *Rights of Man* and the table at which it was written can be seen at the National Museum of Labour History (Limehouse Town Hall, Commercial Road, London E14).

Pugin

The most celebrated of Pugin's surviving works is the Palace of St Stephen's, Westminster — the Houses of Parliament. Barry was largely responsible for the design of the structure, Pugin for the detailed decorations. Pugin's other major project was the Cathedral of St Chad (Birmingham), the first Catholic cathedral to be built in England since the Reformation. Most of his work is, however, to be seen in Ireland — the church of SS Augustine and John (Dublin), St Peter's (Wexford), the convent of the Sisters of Mercy (Birr, Offaly), St Aidan's Cathedral (Enniscorthy, Wexford), the Presentation Convent (Waterford) and the cathedral at Killarney (Kerry), held by some to be the best in the country.

Rhodes

At Bishop's Stortford (Herts) stands the house where Rhodes was born. It is now a museum devoted to his life and exploits.

Ruskin

The Ruskin Galleries, Bembridge School, Isle of Wight, contain a large collection of Ruskin's writings and drawings. Many of his personal possessions are to be seen at Brantwood, his home at Coniston (Cumbria). His drawings can also be seen in the Victoria and Albert Museum, the Ashmolean Museum (Oxford) and the South London Art Gallery.

Scott (Walter)

Sir Walter Scott's home, Abbotsford House (Borders), contains many relics of the author. In Edinburgh stands the 200-foot high Scott monument.

Shaw

Shaw's house at Ayot St Lawrence (Herts) is now preserved as a museum in his memory. His ashes were scattered in the garden on his death.

Stephenson

Stephenson's *Rocket* can be seen in the Science Museum, Kensington.

St Katherine's Dock.

Telford

Telford's surviving works include St Katherine's Dock (by the Tower of London), the seven-arched bridge at Dunkeld (Tayside), and churches at Bridgnorth and Madeley (Shropshire).

Turner

Turner's paintings are to be seen in the Tate Gallery and the National Gallery.

Victoria

Osborne House, Isle of Wight, was the Queen's favourite home. The state apartments are open to the public.

Watt

A Boulton and Watt engine can be seen at the Kew Bridge Engines Museum (Kew Bridge Road, Brentford, Middlesex). A replica of Watt's workshop can be seen at the Science Museum, South Kensington.

Wellington

Apsley House (149 Piccadilly, London W1), Wellington's home from 1817 until his death, is now a museum devoted to his life and career. At nearby Hyde Park Corner stands a statue of the Duke on Copenhagen, the horse he rode throughout the Battle of Waterloo. In the National Army Museum (Royal Hospital Road, Chelsea) can be seen the Duke's uniform and other mementoes.

His tomb and funeral carriage are in the crypt of St Paul's Cathedral. His country home at Stratfield Saye (Hants) also contains many relics of the Duke and his campaigns.

Wesley

Wesley's house stands next to his chapel at 47 City Road, London EC1 and remains much as it was when he occupied it. Behind the house is his tomb.

Wesley's chapel — the heart of world Methodism.

Acknowledgments

The Author and Publishers would like to thank all those who gave their permission to reproduce copyright illustrations in this book. The sources of the illustrations are listed below.

Page 7   Robert Adam   Batsford
Page 7   Osterley House   Batsford
Page 8-9   Victoria and Albert   Reproduced by Gracious Permission of Her Majesty the Queen
Page 9   The Albert Hall   A. F. Kersting
Page 10   Sir Richard Arkwright   National Portrait Gallery, London
Page 10   Arkwright's invention   Science Museum, London
Page 11   Thomas Arnold   National Portrait Gallery, London
Page 12   Rugby School   Batsford
Page 13   Clement Attlee   John Topham Picture Library
Page 14   Clement Attlee poster   John Topham Picture Library
Page 14   Jane Austen   National Portrait Gallery, London
Page 15   *Persuasion*   Mansell Collection Ltd
Page 16   Logie Baird   Batsford
Page 17   Stanley Baldwin   John Topham Picture Library
Page 18   Sir Joseph Banks   Mansell Collection Ltd
Page 18   The Royal Society   Mansell Collection Ltd
Page 19   Lord Beaverbrook   Batsford
Page 20   *Daily Express*   Batsford
Page 21   Jeremy Bentham portrait   National Portrait Gallery, London
Page 21   Jeremy Bentham effigy   BBC Hulton Picture Library
Page 22-23 Labour Left   Batsford
Page 23   Health Centre   Central Office of Information, London
Page 24   Lord Beveridge   Batsford
Page 24-25 "Right Turn"   Batsford
Page 25   "Our Ernie"   Batsford
Page 26   Bevin by Low   National Portrait Gallery, London
Page 26   Charles Booth   Mansell Collection Ltd
Page 27   St Giles's   Mansell Collection Ltd

Page 27   "General Booth"   Mansell Collection Ltd
Page 28   Soup kitchen   Batsford
Page 28   John Bright   National Portrait Gallery, London
Page 29   Dr Bright, cartoon   BBC Hulton Picture Library
Page 29   "Capability" Brown   BBC Hulton Picture Library
Page 30   Blenheim   Batsford
Page 30-31 Clifton Bridge   Reece Winstone
Page 31   Brunel   National Portrait Gallery, London
Page 32   Angela Burdett-Coutts   National Portrait Gallery, London
Page 32   Columbia Market   Batsford
Page 33   Edmund Burke   National Portrait Gallery, London
Page 33   Burke cartoon   Mansell Collection Ltd
Page 34   Lord Byron   BBC Hulton Picture Library
Page 35   Byron at Missolonghi   Mansell Collection Ltd
Page 36   Edwin Chadwick   National Portrait Gallery, London
Page 36   Street scenes   Mansell Collection Ltd
Page 37   Joseph Chamberlain, 1904   Batsford
Page 37   Chamberlain cartoon   Mansell Collection Ltd
Page 38   Neville Chamberlain   BBC Hulton Picture Library
Page 38   "Peace in our time"   Batsford
Page 39   Chaplin and Coogan   National Film Archive
Page 39   *Modern Times*   National Film Archive
Page 40   Churchill, Warlord   Imperial War Museum, London
Page 41   Churchil, 1946   John Topham Picture Library
Page 42   *The Register*   Mansell Collection Ltd
Page 43   Cobbett by Gillray   Mansell Collection Ltd
Page 44   John Constable   National Portrait Gallery, London
Page 44   *The Haywain*   National Gallery, London
Page 45   Captain Cook   National Maritime Museum, London
Page 45   New Zealand map   National Maritime Museum, London

All the pictures in the Places to Visit section are
copyright of Richard Tames.

Further Reading

Almost all the people in this book have been the subject of full-length biographies. The books listed in this section are essentially introductory. Most have been written especially for a school or general readership. Most are illustrated from contemporary sources. Most contain bibliographies which will guide the reader to more detailed sources of information.

Arkwright
R. L. Hill, *Richard Arkwright and Cotton Spinning* (Wayland)

Arnold
Lytton Strachey, *Eminent Victorians* (Penguin)
Asa Briggs, *Victorian People* (Penguin)
Thomas Hughes, *Tom Brown's Schooldays*

Austen
Marghanita Laski, *Jane Austen & her World* (Thames & Hudson)

Baird
M. Hallett, *John Logie Baird & Television* (Wayland)

Baldwin
Kenneth Young, *Baldwin* (Weidenfeld & Nicolson)
Harold Wilson, *A Prime Minister on Prime Ministers* (Weidenfeld & Nicholson and Michael Joseph)

Bevin
Richard Tames, *Ernest Bevin* (Shire)

Bright
A. J. P. Taylor, *Essays in English History* (Penguin)
John W. Derry, *The Radical Tradition* (Macmillan)
Asa Briggs, *Victorian People* (Penguin)

Brown
Joan Clifford, *Capability Brown* (Shire)

Brunel
Richard Tames, *Isambard Kingdom Brunel* (Shire)
D. & H. Jenkins, *Isambard Kingdom Brunel : Engineer Extraordinary* (Wayland)
John Pudney, *Brunel and his World* (Thames & Hudson)

Byron
Peter Brent, *Lord Byron* (Weidenfeld & Nicolson)
Byron (English Life Books)

Chadwick
Roger Watson, *Edwin Chadwick, Poor Law and Public Health* (Longman)
Frank E. Huggett, *What They've Said About 19th Century Reformers* (Oxford)

Chamberlain (Joseph)
C. W. Hill, *Joseph Chamberlain* (Shire)
Harry Browne, *Joseph Chamberlain, Radical & Imperialist* (Longman)
John W. Derry, *The Radical Tradition* (Macmillan)

Chamberlain (Neville)
H. Montgomery-Hyde, *Neville Chamberlain* (Weidenfeld & Nicolson)
A. J. P. Taylor, *Essays in English History* (Penguin)
Harold Wilson, *A Prime Minister on Prime Ministers* (Weidenfeld & Nicolson and Michael Joseph)

Chaplin
Alistair Cooke, *Six Men* (Bodley Head)
Roger Manvell, *Chaplin* (Hutchinson)

Churchill
Martin Gilbert, *Winston Churchill* (Oxford

University Press)
Richard Tames, *Sir Winston Churchill* (Shire)
Winston Churchill (Jackdaw No. 31)

Cobbett
Asa Briggs, *William Cobbett* (Oxford University Press)
James Sambrook, *William Cobbett* (Routledge & Kegan Paul)
Frank E. Huggett, *What They've Said About 19th Century Reformers* (Oxford University Press)
John W. Darry, *The Radical Tradition* (Macmillan)

Constable
Reg Gadney, *Constable & his World* (Thames & Hudson)

Cook (Captain)
D. W. Sylvester, *Captain Cook & the Pacific* (Longman)
T. I. Williams, *James Cook, Scientist & Explorer* (Wayland)
R. Hart, *Voyages of Captain Cook* (Wayland)
The Voyages of Captain Cook (Jackdaw No.20)
The Voyages of Captain James Cook (Jarrold Books)

Darwin
F. D. Fletcher, *Darwin* (Shire)
Julian Huxley & H. B. D. Kettlewell, *Charles Darwin & his World* (Thames & Hudson)
John Chancellor, *Charles Darwin* (Weidenfeld & Nicolson)
Robert C. Olby, *Charles Darwin* (Oxford University Press)
D. R. Brothwell, *Charles Darwin & Evolution* (Wayland)
Darwin & Evolution (Jackdaw No. 85)

Dickens
J. B. Priestley, *Dickens and his World* (Thames & Hudson)
Patrick Rooke, *The Age of Dickens* (Wayland)
Charles Dickens (Pitkin Books)

Disraeli
Patrick Rooke, *Gladstone & Disraeli* (Wayland)
Disraeli (Jackdaw No. 127)

Roy Hattersley, *Disraeli* (Weidenfeld & Nicolson)

Edward VII
Keith Middlemas, *Edward VII* (Weidenfeld & Nicolson)

Faraday
Brian Bowers, *Michael Faraday & Electricity* (Wayland)

Fox
John W. Derry, *Charles James Fox* (Batsford)

George IV
Alan Palmer, *George IV* (Weidenfeld & Nicolson)
J. B. Priestley, *The Prince of Pleasure* (Heinemann)
The Prince Regent (Jackdaw No. 139)

George V
Dennis Judd, *George V* (Weidenfeld & Nicolson)

Gladstone
Patrick Rooke, *Gladstone & Disraeli* (Wayland)
Gladstone (Jackdaw No. 119)

Gordon
Richard Tames, *General Gordon* (Shire)

Hardie
Kenneth O. Morgan, *Keir Hardie* (Oxford University Press)
Hyman Shapiro, *Keir Hardie & the Labour Party* (Longman)

Hill
Alan James, *Sir Rowland Hill & the Post Office* (Longman)

Howard
John Moss-Eccardt, *Ebenezer Howard* (Shire)

Jenner
A. J. Harding Rains, *Edward Jenner & Vaccination* (Wayland)

Kipling
Kingsley Amis, *Rudyard Kipling & his World* (Thames & Hudson)

Kitchener
Robert Wilkinson-Latham, *Kitchener* (Shire)

Lawrence

Richard Perceval Graves, *Lawrence of Arabia & his World* (Thames & Hudson)

Peter Brent, *T. E. Lawrence* (Weidenfeld & Nicolson)

Livingstone

D. Judd, *Livingstone in Africa* (Wayland)

Elspeth Huxley, *Livingstone & his African Journeys* (Weidenfeld)

Lloyd George

Kenneth Morgan, *Lloyd George* (Weidenfeld & Nicolson)

Charles Loch Mowat, *Lloyd George* (Oxford University Press)

Montgomery

The Desert War (Jackdaw No. 129)

Morris

Ian Bradley, *William Morris & his World* (Thames & Hudson)

Richard Tames, *William Morris* (Shire)

Nelson

Tom Pocock, *Nelson & his World* (Thames & Hudson)

Oliver Warner, *Nelson* (Weidenfeld & Nicolson)

R. Hart, *England Expects* (Wayland)

Roy Hattersley, *Nelson* (Weidenfeld & Nicolson)

Patrick Richardson, *Nelson's Navy* (Longman)

R. Hart, *Nelson's Navy* (Wayland)

Admiral Lord Nelson (Jarrold Books)

Nelson and HMS Victory (Pitkin Books)

Nightingale

P. Stewart, *Florence Nightingale* (Wayland)

Elspeth Huxley, *Florence Nightingale* (Weidenfeld & Nicolson)

Barbara Harmelink, *Florence Nightingale : Founder of Modern Nursing* (Franklin Watts)

Nuffield

David St. J. Thomas *The Motor Revolution* (Longman)

Peter Hill, *Nuffield* (Shire)

Pankhurst

Piers Brendon, *Eminent Edwardians* (Secker & Warburg)

Women in Revolt (Jackdaw No. 49)

Paxton

John Anthony, *Joseph Paxton* (Shire)

Peel

E. G. Power, *Robert Peel, Free Trade & the Corn Laws* (Longman)

Pitt

Derek Jarrett, *Pitt the Younger* (Weidenfeld & Nicolson)

Pugin

John Glen Harries, *Pugin* (Shire)

Rhodes

N. Bates, *Cecil Rhodes* (Wayland)

Richard Tames, *Cecil Rhodes* (Shire)

Ruskin

James Dearden, *Ruskin* (Shire)

Scott (R. F.)

Peter Brent, *Captain Scott* (Weidenfeld & Nicolson)

D. Sweetman, *Captain Scott* (Wayland)

Scott & the Discovery of the Antarctic (Jackdaw No. 123)

Scott (Walter)

David Daiches, *Sir Walter Scott & his World* (Thames & Hudson)

Stanley

Richard Tames, *Henry Morton Stanley* (Shire)

Stephenson

C. C. Dorman, *Stephenson & Steam Railways* (Wayland)

Michael Robbins, *George & Robert Stephenson* (Oxford University Press)

Stopes

H. V. Stopes-Roe & Ian Scott, *Marie Stopes & Birth Control* (Wayland)

Telford

Rhoda M. Pearce, *Thomas Telford* (Shire)

Keith Ellis, *Thomas Telford, Father of Civil Engineering* (Wayland)

Victoria

E. G. Collieu, *Queen Victoria* (Oxford University Press)

Dorothy Marshall, *Victoria* (Weidenfeld & Nicolson)

R. Garrett, *Queen Victoria* (Wayland)

Neil Grant, *Victoria : Queen & Empress* (Franklin Watts)

Queen Victoria (Jackdaw No. 131)

Queen Victoria (Jarrold Books)

Watt

James Watt & Steam Power (Jackdaw No. 13)

Wedgwood

Richard Tames, *Josiah Wedgwood* (Shire)

Stuart M. Archer, *Josiah Wedgwood & the Potteries* (Longman)

Wellington

Amoret & Christopher Scott, *Wellington* (Shire)

P. F. Speed, *Wellington's Army* (Longman)

The Battle of Waterloo (Jackdaw No. 18)

Wellington (English Life Books)

Wesley

Dorothy Marshall, *John Wesley* (Oxford University Press)

Wilkes

Hyman Shapiro, *John Wilkes & Parliament* (Longman)

Subject Index